HOW TECHNOLOGY CHANGES OLD LEISURE BUSINESS

JOHN LOK

Contents

Preface

Introduction

Nowadays, COVID 19 disease had brought human more negative influences, instead of it can bring economic recession to global, it can also bring business losses. The question is that when COVID 19 disease will disappear. If this kind of disease disappeared, when global economy whether it can recover again in order to bring our past economy growth situation.

In my this book, I shall concentrate on discussing cruise, tourism and seeing cinema movie lesisure need aspects, to explain how and why COVID 19 disease may bring serious negative impacts to these three kinds of leisure industry consumer behaviors and lesiure needs. Readers can have more clear understanding how and why COVID 19 disease may influence global leisure future development to be worse to compare economic recession, unemployment rate raising, inflation etc. other factors.

How technology invention may help old leisure businesses to avoid customers number reduces, even when high illness environment occurs to influence leisure consumers their leisure psychology to be negative? How social change influences human behavioral change ? Why human behavior may be influenced by social change? Our individual behavior whether can be influenced to bring negative or positive attitude by social change? I shall attempt to indicate cases to explain whether our individual behavior can be influenced to changed by social environment change. Readers can have more understand how and why social change may influence our behavior in possible.

Prologue

Contents
    Chapter 1
Technology how influences human social psychology changes

Human Behavioral network job brings social
economic benefits
    What does human network job mean
    Why human network job behavior may influence economy

Robots take our jobs behavioral and economy influences
    Robot job behavior brings economy influences

Intellectual human economic behaviors
What does intellectual human economic behaviors
mean ?
    The relationship between social change and human
behavior
    How human productive behavior may influence economic development

● New Zealand farmer individual wine productive behavior
● America high technological productive behavior
● China share market investing behavior
Why has any individual country have many people invest share behavior
which can influence the country's macro consumption desire?
Can technology influence human shopping behavioral change?
    Why and how human behavior may influence the country's economic
growth or recession?
Technology how impacts human behavior changing?
How and why employees behaviors may influence economy development?
Robots invention whether they can help organizations to raise efficiencies
or inefficiencies?
Why social behavior may influence organizational strategy needs to be
changed ?
How and why human behavior may influence economic growth or

Why senior age will be main travelling target after COV19 disease attacks to global tourism lesiure need?

What are the characteristics of future tourism industry changes after COVID 19 disease disappears?

How to develop new economic tourism industry after COVID 19 disease disappears ?

How COVID 19 disease influences space tourism industry development

Why does the space tourism leisure need may raise after COVID 19 disease disappears ?

p.81-98

Why does COVD19 disease influences future space tourism leisure need raises?

How COVID disease influences global oil need and price change to impact travelling lesisure industry development

How does price factor won't be the main factor to influence space traveler number when COVID 19 disease brings negative emotion to travellers ? p.99-108

Can COVID 19 disease influence Space travel marketing strategy changes?

Airport service life cycle stage improvement strategy can improve future tourism industry to grow up after COVID 19 disease disappears ?

How COVID 19 disease influences cruise leisure need

How COVID 19 disease influences cruise pasengers their tourism leisure on sea to Singapre and Australia cruise leisure passengers number and medical insurace expense is raised ? p.109-110

Can COVI19 disease cause the cruise industry service staffs lose jobs?

How cruise travelers can protect themselves ?

Illness how influences Online Shopping Behavior Develops

COVID 19 disease how influences consumer individual
visiting shopping behavior p.111-120

COVID 19 disease how brings online shopping
behavior chance

COVID 19 disease how impacts global economic recession
on shopping aspect

When economy recovers after COVID disease disappears

Chapter 4 Technology how helps old leisure businesses innovation
How COVID disease influences global oil need and price change to impact
travelling lesisure industry development
● The prediction of price factor influences space traveler number p.121-140
Can artificial intelligence development to tourism industry
● Artificial intelligence will bring what benefits to
Influence traveler consumption behavior or raising
Travelling leisure desire? p.141-155

CHAPTER ONE

Technology how influences human social psychology changes

Human Behavioral network job brings social economic benefits

What does human network job mean ? Why may human network job be popular? Why human network job behavior may influence economy ?
Nowadays internet is popular to use. We can apply internet to find data , search any new things, even earn money. Why does internet
may become huma network job source. For example, e-publish may be one kind of new human network job. Any authors may apply internet
channel to help them to sell electronic or paper books from e-publisher web store. They may apply facebook, you tub etc. any online
channel to promote themselves new books to let new readers to know whether when they may buy themselves favourable new topic books to read from electronic publisher web store.

Thus, future electronic publisher industry may help any authors to build internet network platform to help them to sell and promote
ot advertise their any one new electronic or paper book topic to let global any one reader to choose to buy their any new topic books from electronic publisher web store easily and conveniently. However, it implies that electronic network platform author may be one kind of future new human network job in our societies.

How electronic network platform author job may bring economy benefit in macro economy view? A person can have few friends, contacts and still be very influential if these few

friends and contacts are themselves highly influential, e.g. one author must not need to know any one reader in global society. When they like to choose any electronic books from electronic internet network platform. They may become the author's any one topic book buyer, when they feel the author's any one topic book is fun and attract they make decision to buth the strange author whose the topic book from electronic book publisher's platform web store conventiently in short time. Although, they are strangers, they do not know themselves , but the reader can understand what it way that made Google from writing platofrm to create new creative mind and typing network job method to replace traditional hand writing book method for global authors. It will be one kind of new human network writing job.

Hence, global any one reader can apply an innovative search engine , such as google.com to find whether whom author personal new topic books are value to read from internet.

Then, the electroniuc publisher's web store may be new book store platform sale network to help the author to sell many electronic or paper books from electronic network platform

in short time. So, internet may be future new network plaform to help global any one author to create network writing job absolutely. Furthermore, internet may be popular social media

to help any one author to build goold relationship between his/her readers. It is one kind of new network, human network job. New authors do not need to buy many paper books to prepare to put in any one book shop warehouse. Their every book can print on demand to reduce out of book stock in any one book shop. They may choose to sell either electronic books or paper books both from any one book publisher web store. So, electronic network platform may be one kind of good writing channel to help human authors to create income and it can also help authors to bring new creative mind and new topic fun content books to let readers to know and buy to read from electronic publisher network platform.

Why does human behavior may be one kind of new human network job to bring global economic advantages. ALthough, it may be free income or without inocme, but the person does the network behavior, his/her behavior may be bring advantages to influence many other people's health. For this case, when a worker in a coffee shop in an airport gets a vaccination aganinst the flu, it does not only helps him or her stay healthy, but also helps the many travellers who might otherwise have been inflected if that workers caught the flu. So, the externality , the result implies the vaccination of even a part of a community conveys benefits to the whole community. For example, governments pay special attention to the vaccinations of school children, teachers, health mothers, and the elderly, categories of people particularly susceptible not only to catching, but also to transmitting a disease.

It is not accidental that governments are heavily involved with vaccination . When there are externalities, free market, fail to persuade individual incentives with society's

their the worker's decision of whether to get a vaccine ends up attracting whether other people get sick. The workers might not fully take all these other people's potential suffering into account when making her or his vaccination decision.

As Stanford University does many suggestions, understand this and tries to help them make the right decisions and so providers free flu vaccines for its staff and students.

Small pockets of unvaccinated individuals can allow a disease to gain a spread more widely well-being. For example, parent weighing the costs and benefits of a vaccine for their child is not always thinking of the consequences of that vaccination to other people. THese are markets in which subsidizing or regulating behavior can make everyone better off. Because the reason for requiring that a child be vaccinated before enrolling in school is not just to protect that child, because each child's vaccination affects others via potential contagions.

Robots take our jobs behavioral and economy influences

Robot job behavior brings economy influences

If one day robots can replace human to do simple, even complex jobs. They will bring what influences to our global societial economy.The popular economic refrain declares that the

global middle class is dying and robots will soon take our jobs, e.g. shopping center customer service jobs, library service jobs, cinema ticket sale jobs, restaurant kitchen cooker jobs,

even, bus drivers, taxi drivers etc. public transport driving jobs, accountant, doctors etc. professional jobs. Whether it is beautiful or petty matter if our future societies have many human jobs can be replaced to do from robots. Businessman must may reduce to employ employees and reduce to pay salary or wage, when robots can be replaced to do their employees tasks.

But, societies must bring unemployement rate rises , due to societies will have many people loss jobs when their employers choose to buy robots to serve their clients or do any office tasks or customer service or cleaning etc. tasks.

In micro economy view, employers may save money in long term, but in macro economy view, it will cause unemployment ratio rises , even crime rate rises when there are many people lose
jobs in societies. These models of doom, though, fail to account for the hundreds of businesses riding the waves of change in their industries when robots may be invented to replace human to do many simple , even complex tasks in our future societies.

WE may image that one small factory needs to manufacture fishes canes to sell to supermarket, the small , cheaper stuff and higher margin parts of the fishes manufacture industry. Before, this factory needs to employe many human factory workers need to help every fresh customer makeing the perfect fishing gear, designed for performance, durability, and cost in order to achieve to manufacture every fish cane in whole fished processing manufacturing stages. Every worker needs to spend about 15 to twenty minutes to finish every fish cane , till to delivery to any supermarket to sell. If this fish canes manufacturing factory can apply manufacturing robots to help them to finish any one working tasks , every robot can only spend five minutes to finish whole fresh fish cane manufacturing process. Thus, every robot can
help this factory save 10 to 15 minutes time to finsh every fish cane manufacturing process. IN fact, time is money, because when every robot can help this factory to reduce 10 to 15 minutes time to compare human worker. Then, this factory can finish about 20 fish canes in one hour if it can use robot to help it to manufacture fish canes. Otherwise, if this factory still use human workers to help it to manufacture fish canes, then it can finsh about 3 to 4 fish canes in one hour. SO, the manufacturing efficiency ensures that robots must help this fish manufacturing factory to raise fish canes number more than human workers. So, in robotic behavioral economy view, manufacturing robots must help this fish canes manufacturing factory to raise fish canes manufacturing number and deliver increasing number to supermarkets to prepare to sell every day. Robots can help this fish canes manufacturing factory bring manufacturing time saving, rising manufacturing efficiency, improving performance and reducing wages expenditure long time advantages in micro economy view. However,

manufacturing robots can also bring disadvanages to society, e.g. increasing unemployment ratio, increasing crime rate,
this factory workers will lose jobs and income, they need earn social welfare from government and increasing government finance pressure in short time, even long time in macro economic view.

Stanford University graduate program in economics, Scott lecturer explained that "in demand and supply economic theory for robots supply and demand case, robots supply number increasing may influence human workers demand number decrease. It sometimes calls " the efficient frontier".

No specific human beings were mentioned in any of economics classes. As robots supply and demand in market case, They (robots) may be purely theoretical " agents" who reached to the most reasonable sale prices in order to persuade any one businessman buyer to make manufacturing robot buying decision whether robots can help him / her to bring how much saving time , saving money, saving cost, improving performance, efficiency economic benefit before he/she plans to reduce workers number when he/ she decides to apply robots to replace human workers in his/her factory or office or any service department, e.g. cinema ticket sale service, shopping center customer service, shopping center cleaning , supermarket customer service etc. service or sale tasks. When robots can replace human to do any one of these tasks in any organizations. So, robots may be human worker agents who reached to prices the way robots would react to a software

command. There was nothing that explained why some people thrived and others did n't or why truly brilliant, hardworking people could fail when much lazier folks succeeded." Having been admitted to the Stanford University graduate program in economics, Scott lecturer hoped to get his answers there.

How robots influence our future social changing? Using the right technology can be a boon to your business in this economy. For internet example, it is easier than ever to find well-matched customers all around the world, to stay in contact with them, and to more quickly design the products they want. If you focus solely on being cutting -edge, though you risk letting the technology
take over what should be very robust relationships with your customers , employees, and colleagues. IN nowaddays society, technoligical advances and cutomation, personal
relationships in business are more crucial than ever. I mean that robots can

not replace human to serve clients to let them to feel more comfortable and passion more easily. For shoe shop case example, if the shoe shop apply one robot to serve its clients to replace human shoe salesperson to serve its shoe customers. Robots ensure that they can not persuade every shoe potential buyer to make shoe buying decision more easily when robots need to contact every shoe potential buyer. The reason is simple, because robots can not touch any one shoe buyer individual emotion very easier.

If the shoe buyer needs the robots to help him/her to choose any right shoe styles when he/she can not feel himself / herself can make the most right shoe style choice decision. The robots can not replace human shoe salesperson to make shoe style choice judgement more easily. They must need longer time to analyze whether which shoe style may be the most suitable to the shoe buyer. Otherwise, human shoe salesperson may attempt to make the most right shoe style choice decision to help any one shoe buyer to chooce the most right style shoe because he/she owns shoe style sale experience, shoe style knowledge, the most important reason is that they can feel every shoe customer individual emotion to touch whether he/she will feel comfortable or happy when they attempt to help every shoe customer to seek the most right shoe style in every shoe customer whole shoe searching processing. Othwerwise, serving robots are only one machine, they can not touch or feel every shoe customer individual emotion whether he/she feel comfortable or unhappy or happy when they need to contact them in whole shoe searching processing. Hence, I believe that some tasks robots can

not repalce human staff to do very easily. Otherwise, robots may bring disadvanatges to let any one businessman to loss his/her customers, due to robots can not touch every customer

emotion to compare human staff in service tasks more easily. Robots serving customer behaviors may cause money lose and customers number lose to the shop in micro economic view.

Intellectual human economic behaviors

What does intellectual human economic behaviors mean ? I believe that when we choose or decide to do intellectual behaviors, then our societies will be influenced to bring economic growth in consequence.I shall attempt to indicate pollution case to explain how and why eithet our intellectual or foolish behaviors may bring economic growth or recession in consequence as below:

On one hand, for air pollution social case aspect example, if we only consider to buy cars to drive for working aimr or holiday leisure aim. Then, our societies air will be polluted. Our health will be influenced to bad. Our car driving behaviors may cause global environment air pollution serously. In long tiem, global air pollution will bring our bodies health to be bad. Although, ourselves car driving behaviors may bring our driving travelling leisure enjoyment and comfortable feeling in short time, also we so not need to pay public transport fare often, but we need to compensate ourselves health economic intangible loss due to air pollution , when cars number increases, dirty air will cause ouselves health to become bad.

In the result, we will need to pay more medical expenditure when we are old age, due to ourselves bodies will become bad, due to we breathe global dirty air every day, due to ourselves cars pollute air in long time, e.g. 10 to 20 years, even 30 more without limited air pollution environment. So, driving cars behavior may be one kind of human foolish behavior and our foolish behavior may bring ourselves future long time medical expenditure absolutely.

One the other hand, water pollution social aspect, if we often keep much rubblish to pollute sea, oil exploration porcessing pollute ocean , ships gas pollute ocaen, then fishes will eat polluted food and drive dirty water, due to global ocean is polluted.

In fact, because human only to conside how to buy boats to carry on leisure enjoyment activities, or catch cruises to travel on the sea. Also, oil manufacturers only consider researching anywhere to find new oil exploration places to manufacture oil product, when their oil exploration processes pollute ocarn . Consequently, global fishes drink polluted warer or eat polluted food. They will have poison. SO, human will have high chance to eat poison polluted fishes, due to fishes are poison or are polluted. So, human is doing foolish activities, we only hope to find oil exploration places to pollute ocean or we only spend money to buy ticket to catch ships to travel anywhere in global ocean. All of these human foolish behaviors will bring pollution to global ocean. On consequently, we will need to compensate to eat polluted or dirty or poision fishes, ourselves bodies health will be bad. In long time, we need have high chance to pay medical expenditure when we are old. So, pollution case may be one good example to explain how and why human foolish behavior may influence ourselves future need to compensate serious medical loss.

All of these human foolish behavior will bring pollution to global ocean. On consequently, we will need to compensate to eat polluted or dirty or poison fished , ourselves bodies health will be bad. In long time, we will have high chance to pay medical expenditure, when we are old. So, pollution case may be one good example to explain how and why human ourselves intellectual or foolish behaviors may influence future long time economic loss or economic growth or recession in micro and micro economic view.

On another water pollution aspect hand, if we often keep rubbish to sea, oil exploration processing pollutes ocean and ships' gas pollute ocean, then fishes will eat polluted food and drink dirty water, due to fishes will eat polluted food and drink dirty sea water because the global ocean is polluted seriously.

In fact, because human only consider how to buy boats to carry on any leisure water activities, or catches cruises to travel on the sea. Also, oil manufacturers only consider any where to find oil exploratin places to manufacture oil products from ocean, when their pol exploration processes can plooute ocean. Consequently, global fishes drink polluted water or eat direty food. They will have poison. So, human will have high chance to eat poison fishes.

Otherwise, such as pollutin case, it can infuence inflation or deflation. Consequently, the reason indicates supply and demand theory. If air pollution is serious, then we will consider health issue, global cars demand number may be influenced to reduce, when global cars number demand will reduce, global car prices and supply number will need to change to fall down in order to attract or persuade global car consumers choose to make car purchase decision.

Hence, global car manufacture number and car price will be influenced to reduce, due to global air pollution issue. Consequently, deflation will occur because when the country citizen usually does not spend much extra saving money to buy car expensive goods. Money value will be low. Otherwise, if global cair pollution is not serious, human considers to buy cars to enjoy driving leisure lives. So, global car demand is influenced to increase , also global car price will also influenced to increase.

Consequently, gobal human will choose to buy cars to drive. Due to we accept to spend extra saving to buy expensive car goods. Car sale price and supply may be influenced to rise up. Money value is influenced to reduce. Inflation may be influenced, due to global car consumers number increases, we would not have extra money to spend easily. Car expensive goods expenditure influences our spending habit to avoid to make car purchase decision more easily. So, human intellectual or foolish activities may bring inflation or deflation consequency in possible indirectly in macro economic view.

On conclusion, above pollution case explain that how and why human intellectual or foolish economic behaviors may bring inflation or deflation consequency as wll as economic growth or recession consequency as well as any goods demand and supply increasing or decreasing consequency. It implies that human behavior may have indirect relationship to influence any goods demand and supply number to either increase or decrease result as well as any goods price will be influenced to increase or decrease in micro and macro economic view.

The relationship between social change and human behavior

Why does economic changes may influence human individual behavioral change? I shall attempt to indicate shopping behavior and staying at home behavior to explain their case and effect relationsip as below:

Human behavior can be influenced by economic change or economic change can be influenced by human behavior? Why does recession may influence consumers reduce shopping desire? In social recession suitation, it is possible that many people lose jobs suddenly, due to businessmen lose many customers. They need to make decision to reduce employees number in order to continue to keep businesses. Consequently, many firms (organizations) their employees may lose jobs. When they have much time, due to lose jobs, they will feel to avoid to spend too much time and money to go to shopping often. Many losing jobs people, they will often stay at homes. So, they will reduce time to go to shopping, then non essential products won't their preferable choice purchase products. Hence, recession will change many losing jobs people their shopping or consumption desires to avoid to buy non essential products often . Usually when economic boom, many people have jobs to do because consumers number must increase when many people have jobs to do. Then, many people can accept to spend money to buy non essential products often. Many people feel spend time to go to shopping can satisfy their purchase of any kinds of new products useful psychology or desire. So, recession is one good example to explain it can influence many people do not like often to leave homes to go to shopping easily. Many people like to stay at homes, becaue they feel worry about spending too much shopping time when they leave homes. Their staying home time is one good negative shopping behavior example. So, economic change may influence human individual behavior changes , they have direct cause and efect relationship in behavioral economic view.

May human behavior influence economic change? Is it possible that human behavior may bring the country social economic change in macro economic or micro behavioral economic view ? I shall indicate publishing industry example. Do you feel that if there are many students feel learning is very important when they read many books or many of students feel interesting to read or they have reading new books in habit, then it is possible that the country will have many students like to spend time to go to any book shops to choose the books, they feel that they can help they learn new knowledge. Then the country will increase students number, they often spend time to visit any one book shop every week. Their visiting book shops behavior which may become their habits. So, the country will increase students number, they often spend time to visit book shops. Also, it implies that visiting book shops behaviors may be their behavioral habits.

So, when the country has many students often spend time to visit book shops , their visiting book shops behaviors may help any one book shop to raise books sale chance. So, the country's student individual often visiting book shop behaviors, their habitual visiting book shops behaviors must may assist help any one book shop to increase books sale number absolutely.

Consequently, any one book shop , its books sale bumber must be influenced to increase to increase because the country will have many students like or feel need visit book shops habit in order to choose any suitable books to buy to read at home in order to raise themselves learning effort. When the country has many bok shops often have many students visit their book shops, then their books sale number may be influenced to increase. It explain why student individual visiting book shop behavior may help any one book shop sale number increases also.

How human productive behavior may influence economic development

May any country which citizen behavior assist themselves country development? It is one cause and effect economic question. I mean that if the country itself citicen can not concentrate mind or energy to choose to do one kind of industry in order to let themselves country can bring the most benefit, then whether the counry itself economy can bring the most serious economic benefit. I shall attempt to indicate these countries themselves indistry choice to explain whether these countries themselves citizen productive behavior may help themselves countries to achieve the largest economic benefits. I shall indicate as below:

New Zealand farmer individual wine productive behavior

For New Zealand country example, this country concerns itself effort is foucs on farming agricultural aspect. So, this country has many farmers concentrate on farming agricultural aspect. May New Zealanders choose to spend time to produce different kinds of wines, e.g. wine or red grape wine is for the people are eating meat, or they are eating dinner.

When these New Zealanders their behaviors choose to do farming or agriculture to grow and produce different kinds of taste of white or red grape wine drinking products job. Themselves grape agriculture behavior will influence these New Zealanders themselves, they can learn how to improve different kinds of grape wine drinking products in order to achieve every kinds of white or read grape wines taste improving aim during their white or red grape producing process.

Why can New Zealander every individual white or read grape wine producers improve their white or read grape wine taste more easily? In behavioral economic view, it can explain that why any one New Zealander white or read grape wine producer can be encouraged or excited or persuaded to concentrate nervous and energy and effort to learn how to improve their white or red grape wine products easily.

In fact, New Zealand is one agricultural food export country. It has good natural environment resource , e.g. land, seed to provide any one farmer to produce themselves any kinds of agricultrual food products, e.g. fruit, or wine food products. Because New Zealanders know themselves country has enough natural resource . So, in common, many New Zealanders choose to attempt to do farming agricultural jobs in order to export themselves any kinds of fruit or meat or wine products to overseas or sell to domestic in order to earn profit.

So, when these New Zealand farmers number has been increasing every year. This country farmers will feel themsleves competition between this New Zealand farmers themselves are serious due to they may feel New Zealanders choose to do agriculture businesses in order to export themselves different kinds of farming food to overseas or sell to local to earn profit.

Hence, when many New Zealand farmers feel that farmers number has been increasing every year. They will feel themselves competition is serious. They must need to spend much time and nervous and effort to research what method is the best how to produce the best taste of white or red grape wine products in order to let local or overseas wine buyers to choose to buy his/her producing white or read grpae products to drink.

Hence, in competition psychological view, may influence many New

Zealand white or reaad wine producers had been beginning to change their learning behavior on researching what method is the best in order to produce the best quality of taste red or white wine products to sell in order to attract overseas or local white or read grape wine drinkers to choose to buy his/her wine products. Their behavior will focus on learning how to raising or improving white or read grape wine taste method more than only focus on producing a large number white or red grape wine products. They believe wine quality is more important to compare wine producing number. So, New Zealand wine producers themselves wine producers behaviors have been changing on concentrating on researching wine quality method aspect more then wine producing number aspect in behavioral economic view.

America high technological productive behavior
For America example, US is one high technological country, it owns many high technological knowledge talent inventors, e.g. computer science inventors. Hence, US must attract many diferent countries owning high technological computer inventors choose to go to US to develop their computer science profession career. Also, it seems that when many computer science inventors or professions choose to go to US to develop themselves computer science new career. In behavioral economic view, due to their leaving themselves countries choice, which may bring influence themselve country job behaviors need to be changed. They must need to adapt US new live. Because they will forgive their past computer science job. These computer science professionals need to spend time to adapt US new lives. They " past computer science job behaviors" will need to be changed to their new US any computer employer's new computer science job model.

Because their traditional computer science jobs needed to be forgot in their themselves countries. They will feel their old computer science job knowledge and behavior needed to change in order to let their US any one new of computer company employer feels satisfactory to accept their new working behavior in any one US computer organization.

So, on the other hand, many US computer company employer will feel that they must need time to accept any one new overseas computer science professions their working behaviors, their working attitude daily, because these foreign comouter science professional, their past computer working behaviors and working attitude must be different to US domestic computer science professions.

In behavioral economic view, these overseas computer science professions, their working behaviors and attitude must be needed to change in order to adapt any one US new computer company itself domestic or local computer science professional stafs themselves daily working behaviors and attitude because these overseas and local computer science professionals must need to team work together.

In behavioral economic view, it is only one way that foreign computer science professionals must need to change themselves past country traditiona daily working behaviors and attitude in order to cooperate with these US local computer science professionals in teams more easily.

Consequently, if these foreign compute science professionals can change their past working behaviors and attitude to let any one US local computer science professional feels to cooperate with them easily in short time. Then, the US computer company itself whole computer professional teams themselves efficiencies will be influenced to raised or improved by the changing past working attitude and working behaviors of these foreign computer science professionals. So, in behavioral economic view, only if US any one computer company hopes itself computer teams themselves efficiency can be raised or improved when it decides to employ foreign computer science professionals and US domestic computer science professionals. They need to work in teams together. They must need to let these foreign computer science professionals to know how to change their working behaviors and attitude to let their domestic computer science professionals feel easy to work together. Then, the US computer company itself whole team efficiency must be rasied or improved easily in short time.

● China share market investing behavior

For China share market example, economic development depends on financial market. Because if many Chinese have interest to invest to carry on shares buying and selling activities in orde to learn how to earn shares interest and share profit when the China shareholder can make decision to sell himself/herself shares in the the high price, then he/she can earn money when he/she can sell the China company's shares in the high sale share price position.

If China has many Chinese like to spend time to carry on investing shares activities. Themselves shares buying and selling behaviors will influence China has many companies can increase fund from many Chinese shareholders in order to have enough money to expand or develop themselves businesses in China in long term.

Consequently, when China can have many Chinese like to attempt to carry on buying and selling shares investing behaviors in China share market. Themselves buying and selling shares behaviors can help many Chinese companies have effort to increase enough money or capital in order to continue to do their businesses in long term absolutely. So, it explains why when many Chinese become shareholders , they can assist China will have many companies continue to develop their businesses if many Chinese like to carry on shares buying and selling investing behaviors in long time in China financial investment market nowadays in behavioral economic view.

Why has any individual country have many people invest share behavior which can influence the country's macro consumption desire?

I shall apply shares market buying and selling investment behavior to explaiin why shares investment behavior which may impact the country's overal consumption desire as below:

In behavioral economic view, I assume that when the coutry has many people have interest to attempt to carry on shares buying and selling investment behavior, then their frequent shares buying and selling behaviors which may bring negactive consumption desire or shopping desire of these shares investors their consumer behavior.

The reason is simple, when the country has many share buyers number suddenly been increasing rapidly. Consequently, these large group share investors must need to spend much time to research any kinds of company shares variations, whether when their share prices will rise up of fall down in order to achieve buying the company's shares in the lowest price and selling the company's shares in the highest price level in order to earn profit.

Basic on this reason, they must need to spend much extra time to research share prices changing behavior every day, e.g. one working person will wait to leave his/her job, after he/she can spend time to gather data to research the day's share price changing behavior after dinner. So, the working person's right time may be his/her share price market research behavior. Before he/she may spend his/her night time to go to shopping after dinner, but nowadays, he/she will fogive to do his/her shopping behavior before dinner or after dinner at hight sometime. He/she will make decision to spend much night time to turn on computer to click on share market website to research his/her share purchase choice to investigate whether his/her share price whether it rises up or falls down at the moment in order to make his/her share buying or selling decision at ever night time.

I mean the when the country has many people are share investors, their shares investment behavioral spenging time which will influence many shops lose customers at might often because the country will have many people feel need to spend night time to turn on computer or watch television to investigate share price variation. So, the country will have many people / share investors choose to stay at home in order to carry on share price variation investigation behavior, they need to listen share market update news from radios or watch the share market update news from computer or TV at home every night. Consequenly, they must reduce times to leave themselves homes at night. So, their shopping behavior also will be reduced. Because these share investors feel need to spend time to investigate share price variation news at homes which can bring economic benefits (high opportunity benefits) when they choose to forgive to leave homes to go to shopping times (opportunity cost) every night.

On conclusion, it seems that when the country has many people are share investors, then their share price investigating behavior may bring negative shopping emotion at night. Consequently, the country's any one shop may lose many customers from this share investor consumer group in behavioral economic view. Hence, when the country's share investors number had been increasing rapidly, it will influence any shops lose many customers from this share investing customer group at night frequenly in short time, even long time in behavioral economic view, because their shopping desires or shopping emotion will be brought negative feeling when they make decisions to spend much time to listen radios or watch TV or computers share price update nes at night. Hence, share market will bring negative impact to influence consumer shopping desire or negative shopping emotion in behavioral economic view.

Can technology influence human shopping behavioral change?
Nowadays, technological development has reached mature stage, whether technological mature stage may bring positive or negative shopping emotion influence to global consumers. I shall aplly internet inventin or ecommerce shopping channel tool to explain whether internet technology can bring postive or negative influence to global consumer behavior in behavioral economic view.
Internet is a good technological tool, it brings e-commerce business chance. In fact, commonly, global has have many businessmen choose to use internet channel to carry on their products transactions between global

online-buyers and their electronic websites. So, global many shoppers had begun to feel online shopping is more convenient to compare visiting shops shopping. Their shopping behaviors have been changed from internet technological tool. Global has many shoppers choose to buy any products from any overseas or local businessmen their web stores. They only need to spend time to find any businessmen their webstores to choose the most suitable products to pay visa to buy from their webstores. at homes. So, in general, global had have may shoppers had changed their shopping behaviors from visiting shops to visiting webstores at homes often.

So, it seems that internet technological tool had influenced global many shops disappear, but internet webstores will be replaced their actual shops on streets. Some of businessmen either they choose webstores to replace shops or choose websotes and shops both or still keep shops only. Hence, internet tool influences global businessmen have three kinds of products sale channels to let globa local and overseas consumers to choose how to buy their products.

However, in fact, many of global shoppers, youngers and olders had begun to accept to buy any products from webstores. They feel to spend time to leave homes to visit shops , their shopping behaviors will be wasted time to not essential part to their daily lives. Hence, since internet technological invention, it had changed many consumers their traditional visiting shops shopping habit to change to buying products from webstores channel.

However, on the one hand, internet creates webstores ecommerce shopping channel to let global many consumers do not need to leave homes to go to shopping. It brings negative visiting shops shopping emotion to global general consumers nowadays. But on the other hand, it also brings positive visiting internet webstores shopping emotion to global general consumer nowadays. So, it seems that global many consumers feel that they often do not need to spend much time to go out shopping. Many global consumers feel convenient and enjoy to choose any products to buy from different internet webstores, when the online buyer chooses the most suitable product, he she only needs to pay visa card to buy the product from the online seller's webstore conveniently at home.

Hence, online shopping can bring economic benefit to online buyers, e.g. avoiding walking time or spending transport fare to visit the shop to go to shopping, shortening or reducing shopping time to do another important matter.

On conclusion, global many consumers began feel online shopping can bring more economic benefits on shortening shopping time, avoiding transport fare spending aspect. So, online shopping will be popular shopping behavior for future long time. It may encourage global many shoppers can make rapid shopping decision in short time in order to carry on any products buying transaction to global any one online shopper in short time easily in behavioral economic view. So, global many businessmen had begun to build themselves one attraction webstore in order to persuade different countries consumers to choose to click themselves webstores from internet channel to buy any kinds of products in short time easily.

So, internet technology had changed consumers traditional shopping behaviors to build positive online shopping emotion as well as raise online sellers' any products sale chance easily in behavioral economic view.

Why and how human behavior may influence the country's economic growth or recession?

When one country has many people choose to do the same matter for one period, whether their behavior may influence the country's pvera; economic growth or recession . I shall attempt to indicate cases toexplain their relationship as below:

For flowing rubblish behavioral case example, do you feel that when the country has many people often flow rubblish on the streets, instead of their flowing rubblish behavior may bring streets dirty? But, their flowing rubblish behavior may explain that this country has people may have enough money to buy food to ear, or enough cloths to wear, enough bottles of water to drink, even they may have enough money to buy new television, radio, refrigeraters , washing machines, desktops or laptops electronic home products from old to new to use in order to satisfy their living needs. So, when they flow old electronic home products, their flowing old home electronic products behaviors may seem that they have enough money to buy other new home electronic products to replace old home electronic products to use at homes.

However, it seems thaat this country ought have many people have jobs to do. So, many of them, they can easy to make purchase decison to flow any old home electronic products and buy any new home electronic products to use . Because this country has many people have jobs to do. So, they can often not use old home electonic products to become rubblishs to flow on streets after they had bought any kinds of new home electronic homes.

In fact, it also implies that this country's economy grows rapidly. So, many businesses can glow up rapdly. When they expanded their businesses, they must need to increase employees number in order to let they help themselves to raise productivity or serve their clients absolutely. So, when the country has many businesses can grow up, it seems that its economy must be better or it is improved to compare past. Due to many different kinds of home electronic products had been often bought to use by this country people in this period. So, this country's any streets can be observed that expensive electronic home products were flowed on streets anywhere. then, this country will have many electronic home products sellers can sell their home electronic products very easily. When this country has many people can find any kinds of jobs to do easily. So, due to unemploymen rate had been decreasing.

In behavioral economic view, as this many electronic home products rubblish country case, we can observe this country may have many people have jobs to do. So, consumption number has been increased long time. So, cheap food, or expensive home electronic products may be rubblish on any streets. This country's people , their flowing rubblish behaviors may be explained that many of people have enough jobs to do, so they have ability to buy any good taste food to eat or buy any kinds of expensive electronic home products to use. So, this country's economy may be improved for this long period. So, in behavioral economic view, when this country can have many electronic home products rubblishs are flowed on anywherer in streets frequently. It seems that this country will have many people have jobs to do, so it causes they often change old home electronic products or replaced them easily, when they have enough income to spend to buy any kinds of new home electronic products to use at homes easily. Moreover, their flowing old electronic home products behaviors also indicate that this country has many people their salaries may be increased in possible from their emplyers. When this country can have many different kinds of home electornic products are sold. It means that this country's electronic home products needs or demand had been increasing, due to many people have jobs to do and income increases to excite their living of needs also improve. Consequently, this country may seem have better economic improvement. We can observe from this country's electronic home products rubblish increasing income in theis period.

On conclusion, this country ought experience economic growth at this period. So, " flowing expensive electronic home rubblish increasing number " may seem that this country's economic growth is rapidly in this period, due to many people have jobs to do as well as salaries increase in this period.

Technology how impacts human behavior changing?

Technology how influences human behavior to bring changing? For example, online share purchase and sale transaction from smart phone brings share investor can do share buying or selling transation in any where and any time conveniently, non manual driving auto vehicle, bring car owner feels comfortable and spends free time to do other matter, e.g. reading, listening mucis in himself or herself car freely. electrical energy vehicle can help car owner to reduce air polluton and it can brings the drivers do not feel drive long time in any journeys in order to avoid air pollution for environmental protection responsible car drivers in our societies. Thus, they will drive long time in any journeys when they can drive electronic energy cars to replace oil energy cars.

However, online technology can also bring consumers can choose to stay at homes to buy any things from seller individual online webstore conveniently. Such as online technology can bring shoppers do not need to spend much time to visit shops to buy any things. They can choose any kinds of products from any online sellers individual online webstores conveniently at homes. Online technology excite busy consumers can make purchase decision easily as well as it can help online sellers sell any kinds of products from internet easily.

In behavioral economic view, technology can change human behavior to be improved, it can let human feels comfortable, more free time ro use, rapid making any decisions, such as apply smart phones to make share purchase or sale transaction decision, online shopping decision, even travelling any where decision in short time, when the traveller finds the most cheap hotel accommodation room price and air ticket price frm any travel agent online tourism webstore, then the potential travel customer can follow the online hotel accommodation price and air ticket price data to make decision when to buy the air ticket from the airline travel agent or make decision when to prebook which hotel accommodation room to go to the country to travel from online travel agent tourism webstores. So, technology can encourage global any country travelers to make anywhere to trvel rapidly. If the traveler can find the country's general hotel rooms and airline tickets prices had been decreasing more sightly. The traveler may make travel decision to choose the country to travel in short time, then he/she can prebook the country;s any hotel room and airline ticket to pay by visa fraom the country's any hotel and airline travel agent webstores., before one week, even one month or more easily. Hence, online technology can also encourage traveler individual frequent travel times to be increased, due to global travelers can find any hotel rooms and airline tickets prices from internet conveniently at homes. They do not need to spend time to visit any airline travel agent to enquire travel choice country's hotel rooms prices and airline ticket prices. They can compare global travel of countries choices ' all hotels rooms and airline agents air tickets prices to make prebook airline seat and hotel room decision before one week, one month even six months early.

On conclusion, online technology can encourage global travelers can make travelling any where and when traveling time desicions easily. It can excite tourism industry develops in long time. Also, such as electricity cars invention can encourage environment protection car owners do car purchase decision easily, because they can choose to drive electronic energy cars to replace oil energy cars in order to avoid air pollution occurs easily. So, electronic cars can increase electronic car purchasrs number, due to many of environmental protection attitude of car owners can choose to drive electricity cars to bring air cleans, even non -manual driving cars can encourage lazy driving and free time driving car owners to choose to buy non-manual (artificial intelligent) cars to drive , because they can spend much free time to read, listen music or do any matters in themselves cars, they do not need to drive cars, robotic (AI) auto driving machine is such one non-manual driver to help them to drive themselves cars confidently. So, non-manual driving cars can attract lazy and enjoying free time driving car owners to choose to buy to replace traditional manual cars to drive easily. Moreover, online share transaction can help any share investors to make share buying and selling decision in short time easily. When they can apply smart phones technological tool to carry on share buying and selling activities easily. They can observe any share rising or falling price suitation from smart phones in any where any any time easily. So, smart phone technology can help global any shareholders to make share purchase and sale transaction easily. So, technology can encourage human makes decision in short time rapidly.

How and why employees behaviors may influence economy development?

In behavioral economy view,I believe the country's any organizational employees behavior may bring indirect relationship to influence the country's long term economic development. I shall indicate past manufacture industry social development period to explain their relationship. For many countries' past business activities had belonged to manufacturing industry, such as US, UK past before 1980 year, it focused on steel manufacturing and steel manufacturing related machine products. So, US, Uk developed countries manufacturing industries may be past main country's economic income sources. I assume US , UK past had one million number different kinds of industries. They ought had about seven houndred thousand number organizational businesses were belonged to manufactured industry. They may include:

Steel manufacturing and steel related machine manufacturing, e.g. vehicle manufacturing, home appliances, e.g. washing machine, television, radio, refrigerate cooler, heater, air condition etc. different kinds of different kinds of steel -related manufacturing machine, they were manufactured from US, UK steel machine manufacturers. So, US, Uk the other three hundred thousand number industry may be general service industry, e.g. hotel service, restaurent, cinema, public transport service, tourism lesiure , wine bar, supermarket etc. different kinds of non-manufacturing industries business organizations were operated in UK, US past before 1980 year.

So, in UK, US developed countries industry development history, they ought have high percentage of businesses belonged to steel related manufacturing machine and steel products. Also, in the past before 1980 year, US, Uk business employers , they employed many workers are manufacturing workers. They needed to spend long time to work in factories. They were skillful workers, and they are trained to manufacturing cars, washing machine, television, heater, etc. even steel itself different kinds of steel related products to prepare to deliver to their shops to sell to US, Uk local or overseas clients.

So, I believe that past UK, US ought employ many employees, they belonged to skillful manufacturing workers, manufacture increasing steel machine or steel related machine number of products rapidly daily. So, if UK, US had had many of these manufacturing factories owned high skillful workers, then their manufacturing steel-related machine or steel both kinds of products number must be influenced to raise rapidly. Consequently, their steel machine manufacturing products would been exported to overseas or would been sold to local both markets , they may be influenced to raise sale number. They (these manufacturing workers) needed to be trained to know how to manufactur these different kinds of machine products in the efficient teams and they ought to be trained to raise their efficiencies in order to shorten time to manufacturing many kinds of steel related manufacturing machine or steel itself products rapidly. So , if their efficiencies and manufacturing performance was improved, these US, UK any one manufacturing worker and their teams ought achieve raising productivities significantly.

Hence, when past UK, US manufacturing industry development period, if these two countries' any manufacturing factories could have many manufacturing workers could be trained to be skillful and proficient manufacturing workers. Then, in past every day to these factories workers, they ought help their steel or steel related manufacturing employers to raise any kinds of machine or steel products number in every team. So, when past in the manufacturing industry development, US, UK could have many factories' manufacturing workers themselves steel or steel related machine products manufacturing skill could be trained to to improve to any kinds of these machine or steel manufacuring products quality as well as their products number could be influenced to raise by themselves skillful improvement significantly every day.

Then, what would be influenced to occur to past UK, US manufacturing industry period? In behavioral economic view, when these two manufacturing industry developed countries, such as UK, US , if they had many factories workers can be trained to improve their skill in order to achieve any kinds of steel or steel-related machine products quality could be improved as well as products manufacturing number could be also increased absolutely.

In consequence, past UK and US both countries ought increase themselves any kinds of steel and steel related machine products number to be supplied to themselves local shops to let local clients to choose any one kind of machine manufacturing products to buy easily as well as they could also export to supply overseas any countries to buy their different kinds of steel or steel related machine products to let overseas steel or steel related manufacturing machine product buyers, they can have many of these different kinds of these steel or steel-related different kinds of manufacturing machine from UK and UK these both countries easily to compare other countries.

On conclusion, I believe that past US, and UK macro manufacturing industry income GDP would increase significantly. So, they would have good economic growth performance because when many of these manufacturing workers themselves manufacturing effort could be improved. So, it explained when employees manufacturing abilities can influence economic growth indirectly.

Robots invention whether they can help organizations to raise efficiencies or inefficiencies?

In behavioral economic view, in any organizations, when the organization hopes its worker teams can raise efficiencies , the organization may choose to increase more workers number and/or it can provide training to improve these workets themselves skills in order to raise their efficiencies. For one warehouse example, when the warehouse increases many goods , they are needed to delivered these goods from the shelves to the delivering destination locations. If this warehouse supervisors feel these workers themselves goods delivery speeds are slow, which is possible due to this warehouse's workers number is not enough. So, this warehouse supervisor ought increase workers number in order to increase their goods delivery speed in order to deliver goods from the shelves to every indicated goods delivery destination in order to let any one lorry driver can transport the right kinds of goods and ensure the accurate goods number to transport to any one client home rapidly.

However, if this warehouse supervisor planed to buy several warehouse goods delivery robots to assist these warehouse workers to find the right kinds of goods from shelves and then deliver to the right destination location in the warehouse. So, these warehouse orkers can concentrate on counting the accurate goods number and ensuring the right kinds of goods in order to prepare to let lorry drivers to transport these goods to these goods of buyers themselvers homes rapidly. Consequently, in the first step, robots can concentrate on finding th right goods from shelves and delivers them to the right goods transportation of location destination. Then, in the second step, these warehouse workers can concentrate on counting the accurate goods number and ensuring the right kinds of goods in order to prepare to put them to the lorry. Consequently, when warehouse robots and warehouse workers can cooperate to work together, the most important, robots, can deal on finding the right kinds of goods and deal on delivering the accurate number of goods of job duty as well as these warehouse workers can only concentrte on counting the right kinds of goods number in order to avoid it has none any mistake of wrong kinds of goods and inaccurate goods of delivery number to be transported to the lorry and to deliver to any one buyer's home.

So, it seems that warehouse robots ought help any one warehouse worker to raise himself efficiency and avoid goods delivery of mistake occurrence easily as well as their help to warehouse workers that can let any one goods buyer feels their goods can be delivered to their homes rapidly. Moreover, warehouse robots can also help these warehouse workers to raise efficiencies because warehouse robots can help them to shorten goods delivery time between any one shelf and any one goods delivery destination of location in the warehuse because robots may help them to find the right kinds of goods from the right shelf in the short time. So, any one worker does not need to spend long time to seek anywhere is the right shelf location for the kind of goods when the kind of goods are needed to deliver to the buyer's home from lorry. Warehouse robots can help them to do this aspect of " finding the goods from the right shelf in short time job duty". So, any one warehouse worker only needed tospend less time to do the counting of any right kind of goods number and ensuring the right kind of goods job duty. Consequently, this warehouse 's any one worker, his any one kind of goods delivery time may be reduced, because robots' assistance and they may have more confidence to avoid mistake to deliver the wrong number of goods and/or the wrong kind of goods to any one goods buyer's home.

On conclusion, it seems that warehouse robots ought may help any one warehouse worker to raise efficiency for any one team in the warehouse as well as the warehouse any one supervisor does not need to spend much time to observe any one worker individual performance for " goods delivery job duty aspect" because their goods delivery job duty that had been replaced to do by these several warehouse robots. Robots can achieve the more accurate of right kinds of goods and the right number of goods delviery job performance to compare any one of human warehouse worker themselves right kinds of goods of delivery and right number of goods of delivery job performance. So, when robots can participate to cooperate with this warehouse's any one worker to do their goods of delivery job duty in this warehouse every day. Then, robots can raies any one of supervisor individual confidence in order to let they do not need to spend time to observe any one of worker individual whose goods of delivery job performane. They can concentrate on supervising any one worker whose goods transport to lorry in the final step in order to avoid to deliver wrong goods number and / or wrong kind of goods to any one goods buyer's home every day. Consequently, this warehouse's overall teams of their delviery of goods performance many be improved by robotss' participatin to goods of delivery task as well as this warehouse's oveall teams themselves efficiencies may be influenced to raise by robots' goods of delivery task participation.

Why social behavior may influence organizational strategy needs to be changed ?

Why any organizations need to know whether nowadays social behaivor how has been changing in order to implement the kind of the most right strategy to achieve the profit aim pursue in possible. I shall indicate nowadays ecommerce or online, customer shopping behavior to explain above question concerns they ought have close relationship between social behavior and organizational strategic choice or organizational behavioral changing need.

On nowadays ecommerce business, or online shopping model, this kind of shopping model in global many young and old age consumers like to apply internet tool to choose any country sellers website stores in order to stay at home to buy any kinds of products from themselves webstores in global societies.

In fact, online shopping model had been popular for long time above to twenty years. Most of global sellers will make decision to design themselves webstores in order to attract global many online buyers to choose to buy their products from themselves webstores. So, it seems that social consumers purchase behaviors had been changed to online shopping from internet invention.

Hence, social consumers purchase behavioral changes may influence any organizations' strategies need to be changed from visiting shops purchase strategy model to online purchase strategy model, if the seller still concentrate on concentrate on considerate how to design itelf , but neglects to considerate how to design itself webstore, e.g. how to design attract product photos to put on itself webstore, how to arrange sale price information location to be putted on webstore and visa card payment location on itself webstore in order to let any one online buyer can feel very easier to buy itself any kinds of products from itself webstore. Then, its potential online buyers will be influenced to increase number when they can find this online seller itself any kinds of products photes and every kinds of product sale price information and visa card payment channel locations easily from itself webstore.

So, it implies that nowadays any one seller ought need to design one webstore to let any one online overseas and domestic consumers can have chance to click itself webstore to choose any one kind of product to buy conveniently when he/she does not hope to leave him/her home to go to shop, because nowadays social shopping behaviors had been influenced to change when internet invention, them it gives another online purchase method to replace visiting shops purchase method to global any one buyer in nowadays societies.

So, if nowadays any one seller still concentrate on how to design itself shop display in order to put any kinds of product on shelf in order to let any one visiting shop customer to find the kind of product to buy, but it neglects to change to choose to pursue another new technological shopping method, such as webstore purchase method in order to implement effective strategy to design the most right webstore as well as in order to attract global overseas and local consumers to find itself webstore easily from website and find its any one kind of product phots and sale price and visa card payment button in order to choose to buy itself any kinds of products in the short time. Consequently I believe that the seller will lose many customers from overseas and local when its other same or similar product sellers choose to design themselves webstores in order to let global any one product buyer can buy themselves any one kind of product when they can pay visa card to buy their products from them webstores conveniently when they stay at home habitly. Then, the seller will lose many global potential customers in long time.

On conclusion, in behavioral economic view, any consumer behavioral social changing, which will influence any in order to avoid customers number loses significantly . In future time, organizations need to make rapid decision in order to implement the most reasonable and the most useful strategy in order to avoid global potential customers number reduces or lose them in long time. So, social behavioral changing environment ought influence any global organizations need to decide how to change themselves strategies in order to avoid customers loses significantly in future time.

How and why human behavior may influence economic growth or recession?

May ourselves daily behaviors influence our global societial continue economic growth or recession? Do they have cause and effect close relationship between human behaviors and global economic growth or recession? I shall apply behavioral economic theory to analyze and explain whether ourselves daily behaviors and our global societial economic growth

or recession which have close cause and effect relationship as below:
Every country itself economic development must depend on any business activities, otherwise, any kinds of business activities must need ourselves business activities or behaviors in order to achieve any business activities as well as achieve the country's overall economic development in macro view. However, any country's overall business activites or behaviors which must depend on any kinds of individual businessmen, themselves employees daily working behavior or activity or performance in order to help them to attract or increase many clients number to acieve " earning profit" aim. So, it seems that any individual business, itself overall every department individual working behavior is one main factor to influence the company's overall business performance.

For agricultural fruit and meat food farming industry example, such as New Zealand is a farming main target industry country. It had had many New Zealanders were daily themselves own farming businesses for many years. Their farming businesses include growing fruit, sheep, cow, pig pork, meat etc. food sale business. If the New Zealand farmer owned a large size farming land, then he will choose either growing fruit or feeding sheeps, pigs, cows to be meat to to transport to New Zealand supermarkets to help them to sell to their farmers meet to New Zealanders in order to earn profit. Thus, if the New Zealand farmer owned large size of farming lands, then he needs to employ many farming employees (farming workers) to help him to carry on farming business daily tasks, e.g. picking up friuts, feeding pigs, cows, sheeps to eat food daily. These daily farming jobs are very important to influence this New Zealand farmer's meats or fruits sale number whether they can be easy or diffcult to sell in New Zealand supermarkets , if these farming workers can own encough farming knowledge or skill to know how to pick up fruits method and make judgement to know whether it is right time to pick up the kind of fruits from the trees , as well as know how feed this pigs, sheeps, cows to eat food in order to let they are better health. Consequently, their farming behaviors which can let these animals can provide the best taste and enough meat from these animals to let New Zealander to buy to eat from New Zealand any one supermarket. Even these New Zealand farming workers can know whether the kinds of fruits, e.g. oranges, apples, gapes etc. fruits whether they ought be picked up from the trees at the right time. Consequently, they can make judgement to decide to pick up any kinds of the best taste fruits to let any one New Zealander to buy to eat from any one supermarket in New Zealand. Otherwise, if they do not make judegement to know whether the kind of fruit ought not be picked up because they still need longer time to continue grow up to increase fruit size and better taste from the trees in order to let any one fruit buyer can feel better taste when they eat this kind of fruit later. If they can buy this kind of fruit to eat later, then this New Zealand farmer's his fruit buyers can buy the best taste of this kind of fruit to eat from an yone supermarket in New Zealand. Consequently, many New Zealand supermarkets will choose to buy any kinds of fruits from this farmer fruit supplier when they feel this farmer's fruits can provide more better taste fruits to compare other farmers' fruits.

Thus, due to New Zealand is one farming main income source country. It's any kinds of fruits and meats need to be export to overseas to sell , instead of local sale. It's GDP percent is very high to whole country 's overall income source. So, any one New Zealand farmer individual and any one farming worker individual working behavior will influence its economy whether it is influenced to grow or recession possible. Moreover, it also seems that farming workers' farming knowledge and skill will influence themselves farming daily activities to achieve the aim of the number of increase or decrease to any kinds of fruits whether they are better taste or the number of increase of decrease to any kinds of meats whether they are better taste to supply to any one New Zealand fruit or meat buyers to eat from any one New Zealand supermarket. So, it implies that any one New Zealand farming worker individual farming behavior may influence any kinds of fruits or any kinds of meat taste because they are transported to any one supermarket to sell in New Zealand.

Consequently, if New Zealans had many farmers can teach god farming knowledge and skill to let their any one farming workers know how to decide judgement to decide when it is right time to pick up any kinds of fruits from trees , or how to grow them on soil in order to let they can grow rapidly. Then, many different kinds of fruits can be provided to let any one New Zealanders can eat the best taste of fruits when their fruits are supplied to any one New Zealand supermarkets. Even, if they knew how to feed foods to pigs, cows, sheeps to eat daily. Then they can be more health and they can provide the best taste of meats to let any one New Zealanders can buy their meats from any one New Zealand supermarkets. Moreover, their fruits and meats can be transported to overseas to let any one country fruits or meats buyers can choose any kinds of New Zealand meats and fruits to buy to eat from themselves countries supermarkets. Then, many overseas fruit and meat buyers will perfer to choose New Zealand any kinds of fruits or meats to buy to compare other countries fruits or meats to buy when they go to any one local supermarkets.

On conclusion, it seems that New Zealand farming workers themselves farming behavior may influence their farming employers any kinds of fruits or meats sale number and income because their farming task behaviors must influence whether their fruits or meats taste are the better taste or worse taste to compare their other local farmers (the farmer competitors) whose fruits or meats taste. If tthe farmer's any one farming worker can be trained to learn how to know to feed animals skill and when is the most right time to pick up any kinds of fruits from trees or how to grow them on the soil methods. Due to these farming worker individual farming behavior may influence his different finds of fruits and meats sale number to be increase or decrease, so these any one New Zealand farmer must need to depend on any one farming worker whose farming working methods, if their farming working behaviors can be the best to influence any kinds of fruits to grow rapid or any kinds of pigs, cows, sheeps animals grow up rapidly , then their sale number may be increase significantly and their taste can be improved to let any New Zealand or overseas meat or fruit buyer to buy to eat to feel from any one New Zealand or overseas supermarkets, then New Zealand's agriculture industry must be influenced to increase. In the world, any one fruit or meat buyer must choose to buy New Zealand's fruit and meat to eat in prefer to compare other countries' fruits and meats. So, New Zealand's GDP may be influenced to raise from any one New Zealand farming worker individual farming working behaviors.

CHAPTER TWO

How to apply technology raises leisure business creative effort

What does brain imagination art creative ability mean ? Can apply new technology, e.g. AI technology to help future any kinds of leisure business to creative new leisure business chance, e.g. space tourism, e-books, online movie, 3D movie, 3D playing games etc. different kinds of new technology leisure activities.

Can we train ourselves brains to raise more art creative abilities? One excellent author, painter, music writer, clothing designer, house designer, dance performer etc. different kinds of art creative performers, whether they use some methods or skills to raise their brain imagination art creative effort or it is themselves owning genius brain imagination art creative abilities from their born or birth date.

It is one interesting question concerns how to raise ourselves brain imagination art creative efforts. Firstly, we need to know whether what brain imagination art creative effort means. In fact, many people feel some art genius, their imagination art creative abilities are due to their parents give them. It means that when they born, they must be genius, any kinds of art imagination creative efforts that they must own, e.g. some genius own writing story creative content ability, creating song or music ability, creative beautiful paints ability, designing clothes or houses or any things ability, creative dance performance ability.

However, some brain scientists or brain doctors or psychologists explain that evidences and experiments indicate may of art geniuses, their art imagination creative abilities are due to their learning more than themselves born to own from parents.

What does brain imagination creative effort mean? Brain imaginations art creative abilities may include many kinds of brain creating imaginations. For musical imaginations example, it may explain any creative aspects of music listening in the activities of composition, improvisation, and performance. So, the music or song writer can own good brain of music creative effort to write many different nature of musical beauty to bring enjoying and listening song or music emotion to music or song listeners.

So, brain imagination may include music or song creativity to any one. But, the differences between good music or bad music creativity may due to the music or song creativity may due to the music or song imagination creator whether who owns what level of musical knowledge, training, literacy, writing music or song experience, or playing music performance experience to the music listener individual listening music or song taste etc. different factors to bring individual emotion response to feel whether the song or music is good or bad after the music writer finished to write the song.

So, any kinds of song or music creativities have close relationship to the creator's brain music or song imagination creating effort had how much. It means that of the music creator owns high level of brain music imagination creative effort, then the music creator ought have enough effort to create many good song or good music to let any one listener to listen and feel their song or music creativities can own unique listening feeling to compare general music creators their common music or song creativities.

On theory explanation, brain imagination may mean that creative thinking, creating thinking is defined as the competence to engage any kinds of brain imagination productively in the generation, evaluation, and improvement of anyone of brain imagination, ideas, that can result in original and effective solutions, advances in any kinds of knowledge imagination , e.g. design a house, design a cloth, design a product, writing one story, writing one music or song, design a dance performance, painting a picture etc. different kinds of imagination.

Imagination may be listening imagination, e.g. song, music or reading a story book, wearing a dressing cloth, living a house, seeing a dance performance. Hence, imagination may be touched or seen or felt by any one. Hence, any one creative art performer must need have excellent creative thinking to create their product imagination, e.g. how to write one good story, how to write a good listening song, how to design a house or a cloth or a product, how to prepare a dancer performance etc. different kinds of creative product imagination to let any one customer to feel their creative products can have the unique or excellent quality to compare other general similar or same kinds of creative products.

Thus, imagination is the seed of creativity. Indeed, there is one fundamental skill that makes creativity possible. Without imagination, there can be no creativity. Imagination refers broadly to the human capacity to construct a mental representation of the which is nor currently present to the senses (Markman, Klein, & Suhr, 2009; Seligman et al., 2016).

Across social –emotional domains, there are a number of forms of imaginative thought, include thinking informed by an understanding of multiple cultures, pretend play, prospection, memory construction, counterfactual thinking, and mind wandering (Abraham, 2016 ; Runce & Pina, 2013). Many forms of imagination, specially imagination about people, including oneself, across time and space, draw heavily on the brain's default mode network, a network composed of several brain regions along the midline of the medial prefrontal cortex, medial pertietal cortex (Andrews, Hanna, Smallwood & Spreng, 2014; Zmmordion-Yang Christodoulour, & Singh 2012, Raichle & Snyder, 2007, Schactot, Addis & Buckner, 2007). Other forms of imagination that involve visualizing, physical objects or physical space are thought to recruit more heavily the brain's executive attention network and dorsal attention network, a network involving communication between the frontal eye fields and the intreperietal succs (Andres- Hanna et al., 2014: Jack et al 2013).

Hence, many brain doctors and brain scientists and psychologists imply that imagination is the seed of creativity. Genius's unique creativities can be caused by their brain imagination. Any one creative product creator whose brain may be trained to own unique creative effort by themselves learning or nay new creative knowledge skills or methods in order to achieve to raise themselves brain imagination creative efforts.

On conclusion, it seems that why any one creative effort is due to creator whose imagination creative effort is due to they attempt to learn new creative knowledge more than their born genius to own creative effort. Many brain doctors or brain scientists or psychologists began to research how to raise ourselves brains to achieve owning excellent imagination creative effort. I shall attempt to explain how we can attempt to learn in order to raise ourselves brains imagination creative efforts in order to become one excellent painter, music/song writer, author, designer, dance performer etc. different kinds of creative occupation performers.

Brain imagination creative effort skills

Can we apply some methods or skills to help ourselves brains to raise imagination creative effort? In fact, many brain doctors or brain scientists or psychologists began to research whether we can apply what skills to improve ourselves brains imagination creative efforts. They had began to attempt to find any one to attempt to do any brain imagination improvement experiments . Their aims to find the best skills to help human to improve brain imagination memory in order to create high level art performers. If one day, human individual brain can be trained to raise brain imagination memory function effort, then many general level of authors, painters, music or song writers , art performers, designers , their skills can be improved to be one proficient art work creator easily. Because if they can be confirmed that one kind skill or some skills can help themselves brains to raise imagination creating effort significantly. Then, when every common art work creator occupation performer can learn any useful skills to attempt to raise their brain imagination creative effort, it can bring much benefits to our societies because when many common art creative performers can confirm to improve their brain imagination creative effort from some skillful trainings. Consequently, we will have much beautiful cloths to wear, good design of houses to live , good music or song to listen, see beautiful drawing pictures, good books to read , good dance performances to see, because all of these creative art performers, their imagination creating effort can be improved significantly. Then , our social cultural level will be influence to raise in long time significantly.

The question concerns whether what skills or methods may help ourselves brains to raise imagination creative efforts? I shall attempt to indicate some possible skills or methods, they may help ourselves brains to raise imagination creative efforts as below:

For dancer performance behavior example, it is at its simplest, allowing your child to thrive though constant play and exploration, uninhibited by the strict rules of science, reason, law or a judgmental society. For any one dancer, it requires an open channel to allow dancer behavioral information and ideas to flow freely into the dancer's space. It requires an open mind and a sense of freedom and limitlessness. So, one proficient dancer needs to own high dance skillful memory to remember every whose dance behavior as well as learn how to create good dance skills in order to attract audiences attention and satisfy their visual dance enjoyment feeling on the theatre hall.

Hence, dancer needs to raise whose dance skillful imagination creative effort, it means that they need to learn how to excite themselves brains to create dance behavioral imagination in order to improve themselves dance skills effectively.

I believe that strongly in the idea of every human action stemming from a complex environmental factors. I also believe an extra ingredient is somehow part of imagination. An internal imaginal word, so such as one proficient dancer case, if she can train herself brain to remember every high level dance steps easily. Then, she ought improve herself dance skills in short time rapidly. So, training to remember dance steps , which is needed to help the common dancer to become one proficient dancer more easily. For dancer case, she may use imagination to recall emotions needed in interpreting a character for any one dance performance to picture an overall aesthetic before it comes to fruition, to invent new artistic dance concepts, to invent new movements to connect old movements , to picture the dancer whose body executing a movement before she has even done the dance steps, to try something new dance steps. Hence, new dance steps and dance bogy behaviors from whose old dance st4eps and body dancing behaviors in order to achieve to feel her dance steps and body dancing behaviors had been improved significantly. It is one good skill to improve anyo0ne common dancer dancing skills, when she can train herself brain to create good dancing steps and dancing body behaviors as well as remember every old dancing body behavior or dancing steps in order to raise how to improve or create new dancing body behavior or new dancing steps. Consequently, she can learn how to change new dancing body behaviors in order to improve herself old dancing skill easily. Hence, any one dancer must need to raise whose brain dance imagination creative effort in order to improve whose old dance skills significantly.

Research concerning the role of memory in imagination or brain imagination creative effort skill issue, it is future interesting brain behavioral research issue for any one brain doctor or brain scientist or psychologist. They aim to help our societies to produce more excellent art creative performers. Most psychological theories of imagination can be seen as theories of imagination consider that " creative" imagination, e.g. paint, writing a story, playing music, designing a house, designing a cloth, designing a dancing steps. All of any these, they belong to " creative imagination". Their imagination is needed to create by ourselves brains. When ourselves brains have clear picture, then the author can follow his brain picture or mind to create a story content, write a song, design a house or a cloth or organize a dancing steps.

Hence, " brain imagination picture" may be one main element to help any one creative performer to create any kinds of creative product very easily. If the creative performer can own good brain picture memory, then his story content can be more attraction, his dancing steps can be more attraction, his house or cloth or any kinds of products design can be more attraction. The question concerns how to create attractive brain picture imagination? Hence, when the art creative performer can have good brain imagination, then he/she ought have good creativity or creative effort in order to create whose new story , new song, new design house of cloth or new dancing steps very easily.

'In fact, imagination pervades human experience. Children begin engaging in pretend play and although cultural and parental attitudes affect the amount and content of imagination play. As adults, we are consumers and creators of fiction, song, story, house, designer, dance performance etc. and we respond emotionally to imagined scenarios. Moreover, we invent fictions even in the pursuit of facts, face of neurological disorders, in defending the bases of our decisions, and in the construction of autobiographical memory.

However, by applying useful knowledge in extraordinary events with heightened emotional content, learners may be better able to access important cultural skills or facts. Consistent with this, researchers have suggested that imaginative engagement might support a range of cognitive abilities, including creativity, intelligences, problem solving, symbolic reasoning, language development , theory of mind, narrative skills, social skills, causal reasoning , emotional regulation , and executive function.

I believe that thinking of new ideas is not an optional exercise in creativity. It is fundamental to learning . The learner must need gather new information in order to raise whose brain imagination creative effort. So, gathering new information is the best method to help our brains to raise imagination creative effort. It is more effective to compare how to think of new ideas to achieve how to create ourselves brain imagination creative effort. For a dancer, if she can attempt to gather any new dancing styles new information from internet channel daily. I believe that she can improve whose dancing steps in order to create new dance style more easily. Otherwise, if she only concentrates on how to think her new dance style ideas by herself mind. I believe that she can not create any new dance attractive style to improve her old poor dancing style easily. Hence, gathering new information may be another useful brain imagination creative effort improvement skill.

Another kind of method is that teaching anyone to new skill. One of the best ways to expand your learning is to teach a skill to another person. After you learn a new skill, you need to practice it. Teaching a new skill to others needs you to explain the concept and correct any mistakes you make. This can improve your mental activeness to a great extent. Next method is that spending spare time for physical activity, many studies have confirmed that daily physical activity also keeps the brain sharp and active. The simple science behi8nd this is that physical activity accelerates the circulation of oxygen on the mind. All of these methods can help your brains to improve memory and raise brain imaginatio0n creative effort effectively. Then, we can improve memory, it can assist us to raise creative thinking or creativity.

Creativity means the ability to change traditional ideas, rules, patterns, relationships and to create meaningful new ideas, forms, methods etc. originality, progressiveness, or imagination. In fact, every one has the capacity to be creative. In the psychological view, these is a debate over whether anyone is born with innate creativity or if everyone who has it has developed a talent. Though some scientists believe certain individuals have a higher aptitude for creativity, many attest that creativity is an actually a skill and anyone can learn a skill. This is the integration of memory and creative thinking at work.

Consequently, we tend to think a parts of the brain specialized for one thing, one particular function at a time. However, neuroscentists attest that all parts of the brain are constantly interacting and building strong neural pathways is the best way to keep all parts of the brain healthy. Finally, I shall indicate ways to exercise creative thinking skills, e.g. changing your routine, you will need to experience anything new or give yourself a new experience to active your brain in creative process. Try changing something small or adding a new activity each day. Thus will help your brain and your body to stretch your creative muscles, or read a book or listen music, anyone of these daily habit behaviors, they will help your brains to raise imagination creative effort effectively. Hence, we can not neglect any one of these simple skills or living habits, they may help ourselves brains to raise imagination creative effort indeed.

Training brains creative imagination effort methods

The relationship between enough sleeping and
brain imagination art creative ability raising level

Can keeping enough sleeping time raise brain creative imagination effort or raise memory? Can enough sleeping influence our brains own more art creative ability, e.g. creating good story content ability, drawing beautiful paint image ability, creat5ing good song or music ability, creating beautiful house or cloth or any kinds of products ability? Many brain scientists had begun to research how enough sleeping time has direct or indirect relationship to improve ourselves brains creative efforts. They also believe that it is possible that enough sleeping time may help ourselves brains to improve creative e and memory effort. If it is true, whether we need to sleep how many hours in order to improve ourselves brains creative efforts. Otherwise, if we lack enough sleeping time, our brains creative e efforts will be influenced to poor? For example, one owning many years writing experience proficient author, if he can not have enough sleeping time every day, it can bring poor creative story imagination mind ability to recreate any new story content in possible. It is one interesting question concerns the relationship between enough sleeping time and brain creative ability research? I shall attempt to indicate evidences to explain their relationship as below:

` Any one must need sleep. If one lacks at least 8 hours sleeping time in the day, he won't have enough nervous to do any matters, even jobs. So , it seems that any creative tasks, e.g. writing stories, painting pictures, designing houses, cloths etc. creative jobs. The art creator must need have enough time to sleep in order to prepare to raise his brain imagination creative feeling to achieve how to design one beautiful house in order to attract people to choose this house to buy in preference, or design one beautiful cloth to attract people to choose his design cloth to wear in preference, how to write horror story content to let readers to feel fear or write romance story content to let readers to feel they are lovers both or write space scientific story content to let readers to feel that they are catching rocket to fly to outer strange space environment to carry on one time space existing journey, even how to design one time attractive dance performance to let audiences to feel all dancers to feel all dancers are performing attractive dance steps or create soft music to let music listeners to feel this music is soft or comfortable to listen, when they are sitting in the theatre to listen this music performance. So, all of these creative tasks to the art creator, who must need have clear brain imagination or nervous to help them to create any one of those creative product in order to let customers or audiences feel their creative products are beautiful or attractive to compare other some creators whose art products.

Hence, art creative imagination must need to any one art creator, if he/she hopes that his/her art creative product can bring more attraction to any one art product buyers or audience to consider more to compare his/her other same art creative product competitors. So, any one art creator must not need to own high educational level of working experiences . Otherwise, they must need top own high level art imagination ability to compare general people. Hence, it is true that any one art creator must need have more clear and good imagination effort to compare other occupation working people in our societies, if they hope to own good creative imagination effort to attempt to create their any kinds of creative products, e.g. design of a house, a cloth, write one story etc. creative products. So, it is ensure that creative art product ought need have good brain imaginatioOn to compare general occupations.

In fact, many brain scientists or brain doctors or psychologists believe that enough sleeping time, it can influence any one whose nervous next day, such as they had attempted to carry on many brain imagination creative effort researches or experiments . They confirm that if the art product creator or art entertainer can have enough sleeping time, it can help the art product creator or art entertainer to create good dance performance, good listening soft music, one beautiful design house or cloth , dancing a good dance performance to compare lacking enough sleeping time product creator or art entertainer. Hence, it seems that enough sleeping time may assist any one art creator to raise brain imagination creative effort.

What the methods to train brain creative effort?

How we can train ourselves brains to raise high creative efforts? Can we train ourselves brains creative efforts by learning method? Has it close relationshipship between ourselves bpdies and ourselves brain creative efforts? Do ourselves brains creative efforts to be poor if we have no health bodies?

I believe that we must need have health bodies, then our health bodies may bring more creative effort to ourselves brains easily, because health bodies may help us to raise ,memory ability, keeping happy and pleasure positive emotin to do any things every day. Due to our brains must be our part of bodies. Our brains are inside to our bodies. Although, we can not see our brains , but we can feel oursleves brains are working, if our memory is high, e.g. we can remember our teachers what they had taught all contents after every lesson. Then, our examination results must be improved because we have good memory . So, enough sleeping time is one good method to raise ourselves brains' memories.

In fact, enough sleeping time does not needed to have enough training. So, training our brains to raise creative effort method, we only need have enough sleeping time in order to keep our brains have enough nervous to remember any thibgs more easily, e.g. studying is one good example for remembering training action or behavior, we can attempt to train ourselves brains to remember any new knowledge from teacher individual teaching. When we learn any new knowledge in lessons, we are using ourselves brains to attrmpt to remember what the teacher is teaching in lesson . If we brains feel tried, we can have breaking time for less sleeping time between lessons in order to keep ourselves brain memory longer time.

In fact, ourselves brains memory and brains creative effort whether they are high or low level, they have close relationship because our creative effort may be influenced to raise if our memory effort can increase rapidly and it can be kept longer time. Many brain doctors, psychologists, brain scientists had researched to attempt to do experiments to confirm that brain creative effort and brain memory effort have close relationship. Hence, many of them begin to believe that if one person can have high memory effort, then whose brain ought have hifh creative effort, e.g. creative story writing ability, creative drawing paint ability, creative music or song ability, creative designing house, or cloth or any products abiliity . All of these different kinds of brain creative abilities , they must have absolute relationship to brain memory. It means that if your brain can have good memory ability to remember or learn any kinds of new knowledge rapidly in long time, then your brain can have high creative ability to be trained to create any kinds of new knowledge easily, e.g. writing fun story, writing fun or good listening song or music, drawing beautiful paint, design attraction of house or cloth etc. any products, even organizing good dance performance. All of these creative tasks must need have good memory ability to the creator, hence, enough sleeping time must be the best method to help us to improve oursleves brain memory or brain creative effort both. We can not neglect to keep enough sleeping time in order to raise oursleves brain memory and creative effort both, if we hope to become an excellent story writer, music or song writer, house or cloth design, good organized performance dancer.

On conclusion, attempting to apply brain memory effort to do creative effort skillful tasks, when one person can have enough sleeping time every day, then his brain memory ability may be influenced to raise or improve. He can attempt to do some simple creative task, e.g. learning how to draw one natural environment scene paint, learning hoe to create a horror story, learning how to create a good listening song or music, even learning how to organize every steps for the dance performance etc. different kinds of creative tasks behaviors. Because when the person feels that he has enough sleeping time, his memory ability may be influenced to increase memory ability. When one house designer, he feels that his memory ability is increasing, he ought remember all prior beautiful or urgue house design in his memory if he is one house designer. After this house designer's prior all house design drawing picture will be remembered again. So, this house designer can remember all his poor drawing paints in order to improve or understand whether how he ought continue to draw or improve his new house picture in order to design his new house design more easily. Because when one house designe needs to spend time to create or design one new house. If he can remember which kinds of house , he had drawn in past in his brain memory. Then, he can avoid to repeat to design his past old house design again. He can use his new house design method to create another new house paint design. So, this house designer can improve his new house paint design if he can remember what kinds of houses, he had painted to design in his past. Then, he can avodi to repeat to design the kind of similar or same style of house again. Consequently, one good brain memory house designer can avoid to design same or similar house again, then this house deisgn may have more house design creative effort in order to design his next new house easily. So, it explains why it may have close relationship between brain memory and brain creative effort.

Can exercise bring more creative effort to brains

Any excellent occupation people who must need to often do exercises in order to achieve excellent performance, such as sportman, doctor, lawyer, accountant, engineer, teacher, architect, singer etc. different professional occupations. All of these occupation people, who must need to spend time to do exercises repeatly again in order to achieve proficent performance or proficent skills. The question concerns whether of one creative art working person who often do exercise, then he/she can bring more creative effort to themselves brains, e.g. one authoer often does imagination to feel new things in order to attempt to write any new story. In his/she creative imagination process, whether himself/herself brain can be influenced to raise or improve or increase effort when he/she often uses his/her brain to mind any new science story scene to achieve brain creative effort or if one musican often uses himself/herself brain to attempt to mind any new music suddenly. When he/she feels himself/herself brain has one good music or song suddenly, then he/she writes down the music or song in order to avoid that he/she forgets when himself/herself brian has this new music or song imagination in his/her mind. So, he / she often does music /song creative exercise in order to improve his/her any new music/song imagination. Can this musician often do music/song creative imagination to bring high brain creative level? For a house deisgner example, if this house deisgner often does brain creative exercise to draw any house design or house picture when he /she feels himself/herself brain has any unique house imagination suddenly. Can his/her frequent drawing any new house picture design behavior, which changes hisself/herself brain creative effort to be raised significantly? So, such as my explanation that it is possible that any exploration that it is possible that any person can attempt to do brain creative exercise in order to raiee our brain creative effort more significantly and easily.

Why do frequent brain creative imagination exercise, they may help oursleves brains to raise brain creative effort more easily or effectively? I shall attempt to explain as below:

Our brains are similar to our bodies, e.g. hand, foot. We must need often do exercises, in order to let we can run rapidly or climb mountains safely or we can swim rapidly. So, if one sportman hopes to win the sport competition, he/she will often run or swim or climb mountains or ride bicycles before this sport competition will begin. So, our brains are such as our part of bodies. Ourselves brains must often need to be done exercises in order to raise creative effort, if we hope tobecome one proficient creative author, drawing painter, house designer, cloth designer , musician etc. art creators.

Our brains must be needed to do any creative mind exercises again and again every day in order to improve oursleves brains imagination creative effort significantly. Any one proficient art creator, who must not be talent especially, they must not own unique talent characteristics. Otherwise, some of talent art creator , e.g. author, musician, house or cloth designer, painter et.c they may be foolish people in general. But, if they can often keepto do brain creative exercises, when they feel any new things in themslves mind suddenly, e.g. one special house picture imagination, one special beautiful cloth picture imagination, one good listening song or music imagination or mind. They can write down to record on paper immediately. If they can keep to write on paper to record any new picture imagination in habit. Their brain creative imagination exercise behaviors, which can help them to train their brains to learn how to create new imagination picture skills, e.g. let them to feel to create any new music or song easily, let them to feel to draw or design any house or cloth imagination easily, let them to feel to create any new story content easily, let them to feel to organize one unique dance performance easily.

What factor may cause any one of above art creator to feel how to create any new creative product easily? The main factor is that " exercise" , due to they can often train their brains to learn how to attempt to create new story content, new music or song , new house or cloth design, new dance performance stepping. When they often use themselves brains to create any new creative products, and write down on paper or draw on paper in order to record their any new creative products as well as aovid to forget their any new creative products. Then, they can revise their past creative products in order to improve their past creative products to be better.

In their " brain creative process exercises", they must help any one of these art creators to raise themselves brain creative effort significantly. Hence, " brain art creative exercise" may be one good method to help any one art creator to raise their art creative skills.

Psychological methods raise brain art imagination creative effort

Can habit leisure hobbies bring more brain imagination effort

How to learn effort in order to raise more brain imagination? Can learning bring more brain imagination effort? For example, if one person often needs any another person writing stories, in his/her reading process can it raise his/her writing ability? If one person often listens music or song , in his/her listening music or song process, can it raise his/her writing music or song creative ability? If one person often watching horror movies, in his/her watching horroe movies pricess, can it raise his/her creating horror movie imagination effort? If one person often sees cloth magazine photos, in his /her seeing cloth photos process, can it raise his/her design cloth creative effort? If one person often sees house magazine photos, can it raise his/her design house effort? If one person often sees dance performance, in his/her seeing dance performance process, can it raise his/her organise dance performance effort? If one person often sees paints, in his /her seeing paint process, can it raise his/her drawing paint brain art creative process?

Some brain doctors, brain scientists, psychologists begain to research whether if general people often to read books, listen music/songs, see movies, see house or cloth magazines, see dance performance, see paints etc. different hobbies, when whose these different kinds of hobbies become leisure behaviors, whether their these different kinds of leisure behaviors can influence themselves brains raise imagination creative efforts. Some brain doctors or brain scientists had confirmed that when general people can spend about 2 to 3 hours per day to read stories, listen music/song, see movie, read cloth or house photo magazine, see paints, see dance performances etc. different kinds of hobbies or lesiure behaviors. Then, these general people whose brains can be influenced to raise more imagaination creative efforts, .e.g. creating story content effort, creating music or song effort, designing house or cloth effort, organizing dance performance effort, creating movie content effort, creating paint picture effort, because when general individual can spend time to do any one of these leisure actions to be habit bobbies every day. Although , they do not be trained or taught from teachers, or they do not born to own high creative effort, but when general individual can attempt to spend time to feel enjoyable to choose to do any one of these leisure action to become hobbies. Then, their brains may be influences to raise writing story, writing music/song, drawing paint, organizing dance performance, design house or cloth etc. different aspects of art creative efforts.

On conclusion, when one general individual can often spend time to do leisure actions or behaviors to be hobbies, then they may help themselves to raise brain imagination creative effort in possible. So, we can attempt to choose any kinds of leisure interest to be leisure hobbies as well as do leisure actions in habit, then our leisure habits will help oursleves brains to raise art creative efforts in possible.

Training and teaching methods raise brain imagination creative effort in possibility

Can general people be trained or be taught in order to help ourselves brains to raise imagination creative efforts? Many brain scientists and brain doctors had began to find general people to do experiments concern whether any general people whose brain imagination effort can be influenced to raise after they are taught or are trained, e.g. learning drawing paint skills, learning dance skills, learning creative story content skills, learning house or cloth or product design skills etc. different kinds of imagination behaviors. However, they discovered that although any one can learn general writing story, writing music or song , design house, cloth or any kinds of products skills, draw paint, or organize dance performance etc. art creative skills, but it does not represent that their brains can be influenced to raise imagination creative effort. The reason is that it is different between raising creative brain effort and raising creative skills effort.

In general, we can learn general writing book, writing music or song, designing house or cloth or any kinds of products, drawing paints, dancing etc. art creative skills or art creative methos by teaching or training methods. So, art teacher may let us to learn any kinds of art creative skills, but, if we hope to raise or improve ourselves brain art creative effort. It is not possible that teaching and training methods both may hepp us to raise brain art creative effort, because human brain is one part of ourselves bodies. Brain is not hand or foot, we can use hand and foot to attempt to do any art creative tasks, e.g. how to use hand to draw one beautiful paint, hoe to use foot to dance, how to use hand to design one beautiful house or cloth or any kinds of products. So, learning art creative skills, it means that learning how to use hand or foot to do any art creative behaviors. We can only learn art creative skills hoe to use hand to draw beautiful paint, how to use foot to dance, how to hand to design one house, one cloth or any kinds of products. So, teaching and training methods can only let us to learn how to use hand or foot to do art creative skillful behavior more easily. These both methods can not help ourselves brains to raise brain art imagination creative effort in possible.

Nowadays, many brain scientists and brain doctors began to believe that teaching and training both methods only help oursleves to learn how to use hands to improve drawing paints behaviors in order to achieve more easily or how to use foots to improve dancing behaviors in order to achieve more attractive dance performance or how to design cloth or house or any kinds of products more attraction, or how to use our mouths to sing more attraction of sonds. All of above these art creative behaviors are only " art creative skills". When we are taught or trained to learn any one of these art creative skills by teachers, ourselves brains won's be influenced to raise any kinds of art creative efforts. So, teaching and training both methods can not raise ourselves brains creative effort. Otherwise, these both methods may only help ourselves hands and foots to improve art creative skillful behaviors in order to achieve how to use hands to draw paints more easily, how to write story content more attraction, how ro use hands to design house or cloth or any kinds of products more attraction, how to use our mouths to sing songs more clearly. If we hope to improve or raise ourselves brains art creative efforts to be any kinds of art creator, we can only keep enough sleeping time every day, keeping habits to read books, keeping habits to see any cloth or house magazines, keeping habits to listen any kinds of music, or see any dance performance etc. different kinds of art leisure activities, because when we can enjoy to do any kinds of art creative leisures when we spend nervous to do these leisure activities in habit. Then, ourselves brains can be excited to raise any kinds of art excited to raise any kinds of arr imagination creative efforts by other artists. Consequently, ourselves brains art creative minds may be influenced to improve , even raise brain art creative effort , due to ourselves brains had saved more different artists whose art imagination of memories.

Brain imagination art creative ability science development

Improvement IQ raises brain art imagination creative effort development

Can we improve ourselves IQ in order to raise ourselves brain imagination creative effort? Do IQ and brain imagination, chich has cause and effect close relationship?

Nowadays, many brain scientists and brain doctors began to attempt to find young people to do experiments to research whether their brain art imagination creative effort cab ne raised if

their IQ can be trained to improve their mind analysis and logic judgement effort. In results, they conclude unique conclusions, their investigations discover that if one young person whose IQ can be trained to climb up to above 100 marks, then their mind and analysis and logic judgement effort may be influenced to raise, even their brain art imagination creative effort may also be influenced to improve in possible. Hence, many of brain doctors or brain scientists or psychologists begin to believe that training on IQ improvement method can bring positive art imagination creative effort influences to develop our brain's mind analysis, ligic, judgement efforts. So, if one person , he/she can be trained to improve his/her IQ mind effort from his/her child age stage till to adult age stage. Consequently, his/her brain art imagination creative effort may be raised to more 50% of his/her general brain art imagination creative effort level.

It brings this question: WHy can improve brain IQ level to influence oursleves grain art imagination creative effort to be raised? The answer is simple that I assume the one young owns

high IQ level, his/her mind analysis and logic judgement effort must be better than general low IQ level people. SO, when he/she owns high level of mind analysis and logic judgement effort. He/she can spend less time to make more accurate judgement to solve any challenges, because his/her mind analysis and logic judgement effort compares to general low IQ level people is higher. So, when the young can be trained to reach high IQ level intelligent young, he/she can make much accurate mind analysis, logic judgement effort to know how to draw paints or pictures to let many audiences feel more beautiful to his/her creative pictures, how to create horror story content to feel readers to feel, how to sing or create the song in order to let listeners to feel

enjoyable to listen the song, how to organize the dance steps in order to attract audiences to see the dance peformance, how to design the house in order to let the house buyers feel the house design is attraction, how to design the cloth in order to let the cloth buyers feel comfortable to wear the cloth etc. different art creative tasks. So, it seems that it has cause and effect relationhsip between'IQ

improvement and brain art creative effort improvement . Because when we born, we must not own high IQ level or high brain art creative effort level. We must need to spend long time

to learn or to be trained to improve ourselves brain IQ level or brain art creative effort. Due to ourselves brain IQ level and brain art creative effort level will not be brought when we born in first day. I mean that we need time to be taught or be trained in order to improve ourselves brains IQ level or brain art creative effort level. Hence, IQ and art creative efforts have similar characteristics , such as intangible, feeling. So, we must need oursleves brains can be trained to bring high IQ level in order to improve oursleves brains art creative effort in possible. ON conclusion, improvement IQ level can be one kind of good method to help ourselves brains to improve art creative efforts significantly.

Creative drawing paint effort brain development

A painter hopes to learn how to use hands to draw any kinds of beautiful paints. INstead of colour choice, paint pen choice, painting drawing quality of paper choice, painting tools factor.

Can the painter himself/herself brain mind creative effort influence his/her paints pictures which they can attract audiences to feel himself/herself paints are beautiful to compare general painters. IN fact, drawing paint quality of papers, painting pens, colour quality of these painting tools factors may influence the picture is beautiful or attractive or not, but we can not

negligent that the painters whose brain mind creative effort also may influence their any one paint creative feeling. For exmaple, if the painter's brain can have good creative house effort, then his/her any house design will attract more people like to see his/her any house design picture to compare other house designers. Hence, this painter ought concentrate on attempting to design any kinds

of house pictures order to improve his/her any kinds of house design picture, due to his/her brain owns high mind creative effort to create any kinds of house to draw more easily to compare

other kinds of things. So, if he/she forgets to continue to draw any kinds of house pictures, then he/she chooses to draw natural scence or human face or human body or any things, such as cloth,furniture etc. paint pictures. I believe that this painter can not draw these kinds of pcitures to compare drawing house pictures more beautiful or attraction. Hence, it seems that an yone painter needs to know that whether the painter , his/her ability can draw which kinds of paint pictures more excellent or more proficient in order to concentrate on improving to draw this kind of paint pictures. Then, it brings this question: How doe this painter know that what kinds of painting pictures who can draw more proficient? The answer ensures be "what kinds of picture image, he/she can own more mind creative effort.

Hence, the painter needs to know that what kinds of brain image that he can own more creative effort to draw the kind of image picture. For example, if one painter feels that he /she has more interest to draw any human face or body paint pictures as well as when he sees any one natural face or body, he can remember their body shape and face shape in his/her brain memory more clearly, even he /she also feel his/her owning human face or body image creative effort is more proficient or excellent more than to create any other kinds of things image to draw pictures. Them I may ensure that painter ought concentrate on drawing any human faces or bodies picture images in order to improve his/her painting skills more eaisly. Hencem any painter must need to know whether which aspect of picture image himself or herself mind creative effort, that he/she ought own high brain image creative

effort on this kind of thing.

I mean that when the painter discovers that he /shw own high image creative effort on matural sene, he /she ought concentrate on drawing trees, flowers, woods, etc. natural environment pictures, or he /she discovers that owning high image creative effort on furnitures, bicycles, books, cups, toys etc. different kinds of productimages.Then. this painter ought concentrate on drawing any one of these products in prder to imrpve his/her drawing painting skills. Hence, any one painter must need to know whether he/she owns which aspect of brain

image creative effort in the highest level in order to draw his/her paint pictures more easily.

Improving brain creative effort future development

Nowadays, brain scientists, brain doctors, psychologists had began to research how to improve humans ourselves brains imagine creative effort significantly. They had began to apply robots to build brains which can similar to human brains, they had been carrying experiements to research whether future artificial brains can be invented to own general human's memory ability, even imagine creative ability. In fact, they had attempted to do robot brain scientific experiments, they concluded that it is possible that future robot (artificial intelligent) brains will have chance to invent to similar human's brain to learn mind , creativity, analysis, memory ability, even future robot (AI) brain development may be improved to exceed human's general memory, mind analysis, memory, even image creative effort level. Hence, it seems that future robots can be applied to do any kinds of art creative tasks. Moreover, (AI) robot brain art imagine creative ability, it is possible that their brain art imaginative efforts can be better that human ourselves brain e.g. creative effort.

Even, future human's brain art creative efforts can not attempt to exceed robot (AI)'s brain art creative efforts forever.

I assume that future brain scientists and robot (AI) brain scientists confirm that robots may be developed their brains own high level of mind, analysis, judgement, memory and art imagine creative efforts to compare human's ourselves brains development. Then, I bring these two questions: Can future robot replace human to do any art creative tasks ? Can robots and human art creative workers cooperate in order to bring better art creative products or robots or human art creative products or robots or human art creative workers work alone can bring better art creative products, due to robot art creative workers are human art creative workers' their art creative products occupation competitors. I shall attempt to answer above these both questions as below:

If brain scientists confirm that future robots (AI) themselves brains can be invented to achieve to own high level mind, analysis, memory, art creative effort, then, they ought to used to do any kinds of art creative tasks in our societies. For example, robots can be used to apply their image creative effort to help humans painters to apply art mind to judge how to draw any kinds of paints in order to raise the paint pictures' attraction ot robots can be used to apply their music or song creative effort to help human musicians to apply art mind to judge how to write one music or song in order to let listeners can feel soft music comfortable feeling or robots can be used to apply their image creative effort to help designer to judge how to design one cloth, one house, one magazine, book, advertisement cover or any kinds of products in order to attract buyers feel the kind of product design is more beautiful to achieve purchase in preference.

I assume that future robot (AI) brain art creative effort development ought be developed to exceed human ourselves general art creative effort in possible. Although, it must be good news if robots' brains art creative efforts may be improved to invent achieve to exceed human's brain general art creative efforts, but it also brings image bad news, they may influence many art image creative workers lose their art image creative workers lose their art image creative jobs when robots can be replaced to do any kinds of art replaced to do any kinds of art creative jobs in our future societies.

Have future our art creative tasks development must need to keep balance between robot's brains and human art creative workers' brains. I suggest that human art creative workers or performances ought not feel robots may be their main art creative occupational competitors. I mean that future any kinds of art creative workers ought cooperate with robots to do any kinds of art creative tasks together. So, robots' role is future any kinds of art creative workers' assistants for one painter example, he can apply robot's art imagine creative mind to help him to mind or analyzie how to draw the natural scene picture, e.g. how to use colour, how to drawing. pens to draw the natural scene picture to be improved , it aims to let audiences can feel more attraction. Hence, the painter may apply the robot's suggestion of natural scene picture to be picture image reference. Then the painter can observe the robot's finished natural scence picture to find whether what this natural scene picture weaknesses are, in order to revise whether how to improve this robot's designing natural scene picture its weaknesses to be strengths to attact audiences' observation or raise their visal comfortable feeling or visal satisfactory feeling to this natural scene picture.

Hence, future robot's roles are only any kinds of human art creative workers' assistants. They can only been given their any kinds of art creative products to let any one art creative workers to refer or revise in order to improve their creative skills from human art creative workers. So, I feel that they ought cooperate to create any kinds of art image creative pictures together to compare that they choose to do themsleves art creative tasks alone. When they can cooperate to work together , their any kinds of art creative products must be improved to increase attraction more easily.

CHAPTER THREE

Technology how help leisure business to avoid illness environment brings negative emotion to customers

How COVID 19 disease influences tourism leisure need

How and why tourism industry development will be influenced by these possible factors, e.g. pollution, travel stragegy, illness etc. different factors to cause global tourism development will spend how much time to experience growth stage from birth stage, growth stage to mature stage, even decline stage. For example, I shall explain how to prove environmental pollution will influence to the country's tourism industry will experience decline stage from growth stage. I shall attempt to explain how and why COVID 19 disease my be the main factor to influence future tourism industry continue development. It can bring the most serious negavtive impact to influence travellers feel fear to catch air planes to go to any where to travel frequently, even sometimes travelling nowadays, when COVID 19 disease confimed had been caused to attack any countries, e.g. UK, US, China, Korea, etc. countries. But, now, it had been influenced to global tourism industry to bring negative impact to influence travellers to feel fear to catch air planes to go to any where to travel. So, global whole travelling industry is declining, Every country travellers number is decreasing, airline ticket sale number is also decreasing, travel agent income and airline income is also decreasing. Many air planes are needed to stay on every country's airport, but the airlines' air planes, they are needed to pay parking rent to airport. So, expenditure is very much to any airlines.

Why COV19 disease and traveller traveelling lesiure behavior have close relationship ?

Psychological method to predict travel behavioural consumption.

On the psychological view point, I think individual traveler's character will have those kind of personal characteristics. First, simplicity searchers value above everything ease not transparency in their travel planning and holiday making, and are willing to avoid having to go through extensive research. Second, cultural purists use their travel as an opportunity to immerse themselves in an unfamiliar looking to break themselves entirely from their home lives and engage. Sincerely with a different way of living. Third, social capital seekers understand that to be well travelled is a personal quality, and their choices are shaped by their desire to take maximum of social reward from their travel. They will exploit the potential of digital media to enrich and inform their experiences, and structure their adventures always keeping in mind they are being watched by online audiences. Finally, reward hunters seek a return on the investment who make in their busy , high-achieving lives. Linked in part to the growing trend of wellness, including both physical and mental self improvement who seek truly extraordinary and often indulgent or luxurious' must have experiences.

Why needs to know the personal character of individual traveler's characteristics? Because if travel agents could feel which kinds of individual traveler's character, then who can predict which kind of travel package to design to them more easily. For example, how to determine future travel behaviour from past travel experience and perceptions of risk and safety? We need to concern that the influences of past international travel experience, types of risk associated with international travel and the overall degree of safety feeling during international travel on individual's travelling experiences likelihood of travelling to various geographic regions on their next international vacation trip or avoidance of those regions, due to perceived risk. Because individual traveler's experience of safety risk degree to the countries, it will influence who chooses to go to the countries/ country to travel again.

Why COVID 19 disease influences travellers begin to concern green or nature tourism ?

However, green or nature tourism strategy may include these elements : Quality, tourism should have an impact on the quality of life for all members of the tourist process, exploitation of nature resources should be optimal and ensure their generation, balance, distribution of benefits among participants in the tourist process must be fair. So, future any kinds of green or nature tourism will need have these features in order to attract many travelers to visit any countries' green lands, e.g. they may rent cars to travel to green lands. So, developing attractive green lands will be one kind new travelling trend for green tourism in global future travel market.

There are two types of models that contribute to the better understanding of future tourism industry development, explanatory model refer to factors that cause development growth. For example, whether the travelers feel necessary to travel to different destinations, very often nice landscapes and sightseeing, pescriptive modes (e.g. life clcle explanations, physical models) examines tourism from what appears on ground e.g. large hotels facilities etc. Hence, any kinds of tourism leisure must need build these both models in order to attract travelers to choose to buy the tourism package from the travel agent more easily. It is important tourism leisure element to any one travel agent's tourism service package if it hopes to develop its tourism service success. So, the expansion of the tourist region over the natural boundaries of the city centre that occured in the first place as a result of the growth of tourism demand, is the end causing this very expansion to continue.

Butler (1980) involves a six stage evoluation of tourism, namely explanation, involvement, development, consolidation, stagnation, and post-stagnation. The last stage is further characterized by a period of decline, rejuvenation or stabilization. The applicability of the model to a given area has been assessed and judged of a tourist destination's development matched the six phases conceptually described by Butler
reference
Butler, R.W. (1980). the concept of a tourist area cycle of evolution: Implications for management of resources. Canadian Geographer, 24, 5-12.
Hence, our tourism industry is facing decline life cycle stage because COVD 19 human mouth disease has influenced many travelers feel fear to catch airplanes to travel, even they also feel to contact the potential COVD 19 human mouth disease people when they arrive the country , they feel that they may contact these sick people, instead of airplanes. So, this kind disease had influenced many travel agents reduce tourism service package

number , due to many travelers' tourism leisure activities will reduce, due to travelers number reduces, they only carry cargos to transport to replace travelers COVD 19 disease influence our tourism industry is experiencing decline life cycle stage nowadays. Unless, COVD 19 human mouth attacking to lung disease can be treated by new medicine invention . Otherwise, tourism industry can not re-grow to mature life cycle stage easily.

The most used framework for examing stagnation and possible decline in tourism destinations has been tourist area life cycle model (Butler, 1980). The model has been operationalized frequently in the tourism lierature. It includes series of stages in tourism development, leadning eventually to the stagnation and post-stagnation stages. When a nature destination can either decline, however, it does not offer a systematic explanation of hoe tourism destination might avoid decline . Such as COVD 19 human mouth disease may influence travelers feel fear to catch air planes. So, even the country has beautiful nature scene to attract people to travel, althoug it is a nature attractive destination, but due to COVD19 disease occurs, it may influence this country's this nature attractive destination to enter decline life cycle stage at this moment.

Hence, tourism industry's life cycle stage , sometime it can be influenced by non predicted factor, such as COVD19 disease factor, it can influence travelers' travelling desire to be reduced suddenly from 2019 , due to they feel afraid to catch air planes to avoid to get this kind COVD 19 human mouth disease to bring lung disease when they are sitting in closed window inside air plane environment. So, COVD 19 human counth disease causes global tourism industry is facing serious decline life cycle stage. The question is that any one does not know when this kind COVD 19 disease will be treated by new medicine invention, so if this kind COVD 19 disease still can not be killed by new medicine invention, then it will continue to influence global tourism development to be improved , even any nature attractive scenes, they can not persuade any travelers to catch air planes to visit any countries to travel easily. But, however, we still need to keep our natural environment to prepare future COVD 19 diease disappears , e.g. parks are important places for the protection of ecological systems and natural resources as well as for the provision ot recreational and tourism opportunities for the public. Then, nature or green tourism can be continue to develop to attract many travelers to travel after COVD 19 disease disappears in the future.

How COVID 19 disease influences tourism industry recession ?

Butler , R.W. (1980)'s model begins with a discovery and exploration or birth stage in which a location is discovered by a small, select group of people as a place with desirable assets often, this discovery is nature population who may see the perceived assets. As just ordinary aspects of their environment or local culture. The early tourists have very little support in the form of amenities, and typically, this is preferred and is part of a location's of being undiscovered. The early tourists, therefore rely heavily on and interact frequently with the residents of the region. This small group of early tourists is largely in dependent and shares information about a destination by word of mouth or by select affinity groups. Over time, as more people are introduced to the destination, the number of visitors begins to increase. So " word of mouth" will be traveler information to persuade them to make travelling destination choices in the tourism industry beginning. It is tourism industry's birth life cycle stage characteristics . However, internet invention can let any one see any countries' scene photos, so it is one kind of good advertisement method to introduce any countries' scene, instead of travelling magazine in tourism growth and maturity life cucle both stages.

Why senior age will be main travelling target after COV19 disease attacks to global tourism lesiure need?

In the past, Germany government had established tourism survey analysis to analyze survey data in order to arrive at reliable conclusions on future trends in travel behavior. To aim to find how demographic change will influence the tourism market and how the industry can adapt to those changes. The travel analysis provided data on tourism consumer behavior, including attitudes, motives and intentions. Since, 1970 year, it is based on a random sample, representative for the population in private households aged 14 years or older. Then, a continuous high scientific standard combined with a national and international users makes the travel analysis a useful tool and reliable source for tourism industry and policy decisions. It aimed to gather statistical data. e.g. on the age structure and on demographic trends, quantitative and qualitative analysis with time series data from the travel analysis. It shows e.g. not only the future volume , quite different from today's seniors, or how who will travel of family holidays will change, e.g. single parents of low, but grandparents of growing significance for tourism.

Demographic change is said to be one of the important drivers for new trends in consumer traveling change behavior in most European countries (e.g. Lind 2001). Because the growing number of senior citizens in the European Union and other industralised countries, such as the USA and Japan, looks to become one of the major marketing challenges for the tourism industry. United Nations statistics predict that the share of people being 60 age or older will grow dramatically in the coming future, and is expected to rise from 10 percent of the world population in 2000 year to more than 20 percent in 2050 year (United Nations Population Division, 2001). From its statistic, some data showed that travel propensity increased throughout life until the age of about 50 years of age and was then kept stable until very late in life 75 age. The most important results is that the travel propensity when getting older is not going down between 65 and 75 age of course, the overall development of this variable is influenced by a lot of other factors which are rsponsible for quite a variation over time. It is now possible to suggest that the general pattern of travel propensity is one of the key indicators for holiday life cycle travel behaviour, includes three stages. The growth stage tends to increase from early aduithood until 45 age old or when reaching some 80%. The next stage is stabilisation from the ages of around 50 age, until 75 age old, starting with a lower increase. Finally, the decrease stage is a slight decrease occurs once people reach the more advanced age of 75 age to 85 age old (Lohmann & Danielsson 2001).

So, it seems Germany government tourism prediction to future travellers' behaviour indicated these findings, such as on how future senior generations will travel, who had used survey data to examine the patterns of travel behaviour of a generation getting older and applied the findings to draw conclusions on the future. Also, it predicted that on the future of family trips, family semgmentation will be the travel behaviour patterns in the future. These findings together with the statistical data on demographic change allowed for a better understanding of the coming tends in family holidays. It's aim developed in consumer behaviour related to demographic change and predicted what will happen future of tourism one had to consider other influences and drivers as well, for example, trends on the supply side. e.g. low cost airlines or in travelling consumption behaviour in general whether how the past may provide a key to predict travel patterns of senior sitizens to the future.

Given the projected growth of the senior citizens market, designing specific marketing strategies to meet the prospective needs of elderly tourists will become increasingly important. It has been an implict assumption that it will be a close relationship between the travel behaviour of today's senior citizens and the those of future ones. The growing number of senior citizens in the world. e.g. China, Hong Kong, Japan, USA etc. countries. Global senior citizen tourism market will be based solely on demographic predictions about the future of the population's age structure. However, many of these seniors won't only live longer but will be fitter and more active until later in life. Many of the will also have plenty in life. Many of them will also have plenty of time and money to spend on travel. So, will these new seniors behave like today's senior citizens? Will they adopt the same travel behaviour as the previous generation or become a new market of oldies for the leisure and tourism indudtry? However, to determine the actual number of senior citizens who will be travelling and to sought to evaluate and specify certain difficult to predict the actual numbers of senior citizen to any country. However, they can be based on the implicit assumption that there is a close relationship between the travel behaviour of past, present and future seniors. But is this a valid assumption? As the reiseanalyse travel analysis survey, which was conducted in Germany every year, offered some interesting data possibiltieis. It was designed to monitor the holiday travel behaviour, opinions and attitudes of Germans and has been carried out since 1970 year, questions in the questionnaire. Data are based on face to face interviews, with a representative sample of more than 7,500 repondents, the interviews being carried out in January each year. All results refer to the average for the defined generated, which ranges generally over ten years. The group of people then at the age of 60 to 69 age is described. This corresponds to the same generation ten years ago, when they had an age of 50 to 59 age. When this methodological approach is not necessarily very sophisticated, it does have the important advantages of being cost effective. Thus, COVD19 disease can influence future senior age traveller personal tourism leisure need raise, because they may feel COVID 19 disease can not be caused to disappear in short time. They are fear death, so they will choose to go to any where to travel before they die. So, future global tourism industry's main customer target may be old age people more than young age people.

Hence, our tourism industry is facing decline life cycle stage because COVD 19 human mouth disease has influenced many travelers feel fear to catch airplanes to travel, even they also feel to contact the potential COVD 19 human mouth disease people when they arrive the country , they feel that they may contact these sick people, instead of airplanes. So, this kind disease had influenced many travel agents reduce tourism service package number , due to many travelers' tourism leisure activities will reduce, due to travelers number reduces, they only carry cargos to transport to replace travelers COVD 19 disease influence our tourism industry is experiencing decline life cycle stage nowadays. Unless, COVD 19 human mouth attacking to lung disease can be treated by new medicine invention . Otherwise, tourism industry can not re-grow to mature life cycle stage easily.

The most used framework for examing stagnation and possible decline in tourism destinations has been tourist area life cycle model (Butler, 1980). The model has been operationalized frequently in the tourism lierature. It includes series of stages in tourism development, leadning eventually to the stagnation and post-stagnation stages. When a nature destination can either decline, however, it does not offer a systematic explanation of hoe tourism destination might avoid decline . Such as COVD 19 human mouth disease may influence travelers feel fear to catch air planes. So, even the country has beautiful nature scene to attract people to travel, althoug it is a nature attractive destination, but due to COVD19 disease occurs, it may influence this country's this nature attractive destination to enter decline life cycle stage at this moment.

Hence, tourism industry's life cycle stage , sometime it can be influenced by non predicted factor, such as COVD19 disease factor, it can influence travelers' travelling desire to be reduced suddenly from 2019 , due to they feel afraid to catch air planes to avoid to get this kind COVD 19 human mouth disease to bring lung disease when they are sitting in closed window inside air plane environment. So, COVD 19 human counth disease causes global tourism industry is facing serious decline life cycle stage. The question is that any one does not know when this kind COVD 19 disease will be treated by new medicine invention, so if this kind COVD 19 disease still can not be killed by new medicine invention, then it will continue to influence global tourism development to be improved , even any nature attractive scenes, they can not persuade any travelers to catch air planes to visit any countries to travel easily. But, however, we still need to keep our natural environment to prepare future COVD 19 diease disappears , e.g. parks are important places for the protection of ecological systems and natural resources as well as for the provision ot recreational and tourism opportunities for the public. Then, nature or green tourism can be continue to develop to attract many travelers to travel after COVD 19 disease disappears in the future.

● What are the characteristics of future tourism industry changes after COVID 19 disease disappears?

Butler , R.W. (1980)'s model begins with a discovery and exploration or birth stage in which a location is discovered by a small, select group of people as a place with desirable assets often, this discovery is nature population who may see the perceived assets. As just ordinary aspects of their environment or local culture. The early tourists have very little support in the form of amenities, and typically, this is preferred and is part of a location's of being undiscovered. The early tourists, therefore rely heavily on and interact frequently with the residents of the region. This small group of early tourists is largely in dependent and shares information about a destination by word of mouth or by select affinity groups. Over time, as more people are introduced to the destination, the number of visitors begins to increase. So " word of mouth" will be traveler information to persuade them to make travelling destination choices in the tourism industry beginning. It is tourism industry's birth life cycle stage characteristics . However, internet invention can let any one see any countries' scene photos, so it is one kind of good advertisement method to introduce any countries' scene, instead of travelling magazine in tourism growth and maturity life cucle both stages.

Moreover, space tourism is at the birth life cycle stage. It needs travelers feel interest to travel space, if this kind space tourism service providers hope to implement their any space journeys in success. These factors may influence its development succeeds. Nowadays, its target market is wealthy travelers group, wealthy individual are needed, as they serve as the main consumers for space tourism . For space tourism to succeed there must be enough demand from those who are able to afford to expensive ticket. To date there have only been seven commercial space travelers, or space tourists, although they prefer to be called space flight participant, as they see themselves as pioneers and adventers as opposed to ordinary tourists. So, any future space tourism that price must need to reduce to general public, e.g. ordinary income level people, they can spend, if space tourism hopes to reach from stage stage rapidly. So, space tourism is still far to mature stage.It depends on whether how long time its any space journey ticket price can be reduced to any one can pay. So, when its customer target is not only wealthy travelers, many ordinary or common income level people, they can pay to any one space jounrney. It may mean to reach growth life cycle stage.

Chapter 2

How COVID 19 disease bring space tourism industry development

● The space tourism leisure need may raise after COVID 19 disease disappears

When human space tourism of commericalization of activities in outer space can bring these feeling to let any one space traveler feels then, it may mean that it can reach growth stage, such as they may feel their any space journeys may bring positive impacts that outer. Space recreation can produce, in order to come up with space tourism, exploring and untravelling the hidden anystories of the space are needed. Also they can feel need drastically broadens and enrichs human's technical awareness and constructive knowledge need from any one space tourism journey package. When space tourism reachs mature life cycle stage? What its characteristics are? When any one space travelers can feel that not only earth based attractions that simulate the space experience , they must need to catch airships to experience this different tourism experience, such as space theme parks, space training camps, virtual reality facilities , space hotels (skotel), multimedia interactive games and tele robotic moon rovers controlled from earth, but also parabolic flights, lasting up to three days or week long stay at floating space hotel, including participatory educational ,as well as sports competitions (i.e. space olympics). Hence, above these will be nay space tourism development. It can reach mature life cycle stage characteristics when any one can feel the real travelling mouth to compare to travel our earth anywhere, they can not find that they feel space tourism may be same to our earth's holiday (need to rela) or cultural (know different places or specialized tourism, e.g. expectations of adventures , even space scientists discover new experiences to expectations of adventure or get more information, scientific interest feeling. Then, at this moment, we can call space tourism has reached the mature stage. However, I believe that to develop space tourism in success. We must need to control space tourism ticket price to be reduced to general low income people. They may spend budget level. So, ticket price may be one major factor to influence future space tourism growth when it can reach mature stage. Also, it mean that whether space tourism may become another kind of popular tourism lesiure activities to use. It depends on ticket price factor, instead of its any space tourism trip arrangement factor. So, any one space tourism service provider must need long time to spend in order to implement its different strategies, e.g. ticket price, space trip arrangemet to achieve its their space tourism to achieve its their space tourism different destination package in success if they hope their future space tourism business can grow up in short time.

Why does COVD19 disease influences future space tourism leisure need raises?

● Psychology and economic environment changing both factors influence whole space tourism market leisure desire

How can psychology method predict space tourism leisure desire? I believe that it has relationship between the space tourism planner and the economic environment as well as his/her psychology as below:

Firstly, on the economic environment influence hand, it includs these both economic situations, either in the good economic environment, many people can earn high income and employers can supply many job number to provide to many people to work, then it will influence the space travelling planner has more space travelling desire. Otherwise, or in the bad economic, less people can earn high income and employers can not supply many job number to provide to many people to work, it will influence the space travelling planner has less space travelling desire.

Secondly, on these both the space travelling planner individual psychology influence hand, the space travelling planner will have these both aspects of individual psychological influence, it includes these both either positive or negative psychological influence aspectsas below:

On the positive psychological influence aspect, if the space travelling planner has confidence to the space travelling leisure company can provide safe, comfortable, good quality of one space travelling trip arrangement, good taste food arrangement, reasonable space ticket price and every reasonable space trip for space hotel living arrangement and space garden and space farming land visiting journey arrangement, even, space swimming pool and space sport centre and space cinema leisure arrangement to let whom to stay on the planet at least one day trip, it means not one short time space trip, e.g. the spacecraft only flies about half hour or one half. It can not fly to the planet to arrive its space station destination to stay to let the space travelling planner to live at the space hotel at least one night. Then the space travelling planner will have more desire to choose to catch the space tourism leisure company's spacecraft to travel to space. Otherwise, on the negative psychological influence aspect, if the space travelling planner lacks confidence to the space travelling leisure company can provide safe, comfortable, good quality of one space travelling trip arrangement, good taste food arrangement, reasonable space ticket price and every reasonable space trip for space hotel living arrangement and space garden and space farming land visiting journey arrangement, even, space swimming pool and space sport centre and space cinema leisure arrangement to let whom to stay on the planet at least one day trip, it means not one short time space trip, e.g. the spacecraft only flies about half hour or one half. It can not fly to the planet to arrive its space station destination to stay to let the space travelling planner to live at the space hotel at least one night. Then the space travelling planner will have less desire to choose to catch the space tourism leisure company's spacecraft to travel to space.

Hence, it seems economic environment changing factor and the space travelling planner's confidence factor to the space tourism leisure providers will influence the whole space travelling market whose space travelling consumer's space travelling leisure consumption desire to be more or less. So, any one space tourism provider can not neglect these both factors how to influence whose customer consumption desire.

● space tourism strategy

Future any space tourism leisure business needs have good business plan to outline the space tourism leisure business in these aspects , such as: different space tourism destinations of every space tourism journey, technical , financial and regulatory factors for growing space tourism leisure consumption into any one kind of unique artificial intelligent space tourism journey for identified passenger target group.

All how to design one space tourism business development plan to attempt to predict whether what trends will influence how every different kinds of identified space tourism journey in order to achieve passenger number growing aim as well as how to achieve one attractive space tourism leisure to satisfy future space tourism passenger individual space travel needs more easily.

I shall indicate what aspects to future every space tourism traveler who will consider in order to reduce the space tourism traveler personal worry to catch any pace boats to leave our Earth to fly to other planets to travel.

I recommend that any space tourism leisure organizations need to concern these aspects in their space tourism leisure business plan as below:

(1) safe space tourism journey

On first aspect concerns safe space tourism journey plan to let all space tourism travelers will considerate safe issue. They must ensure space boats that is safe to catch them to fly to planets in their space journeys. So, any space tourism leisure business will utilize previous flight rated and proven technologies to form the basis for manufacturing spacecraft vehicles, and will incorporate the latest modern avionics and flight systems for ensuring safety, reliability and economical operation in order to reduce any space tourism traveler personal worry to catch any spacecraft.

So, the space tourism safe journey plan is one very important factor to influence space tourism consumer number for them if any one of space tourism leisure business hoped they can grow the space tourism consumer number for long term. For example, the space boat flight hardware must often be maintained at the space station. It is needed to be considered by space boat experts as risky, extremely expensive and potentially sensitive. To aims to ensure spacecraft will offer an economical and safe alternative for any satellite manufacturers and other space tourism entertainment organizations have a desire or requirement for space tourism flight.

(2) reduction cost expense plan

On second aspect concerns reduction cost expense plan, any space tourism entertainment organizations need have the experience and capacity for safely launching a fully loaded , including space tourism passengers and passenger individual cargo for every spacecraft tourism journey. As a result of outsourcing the launch role to a major contractor, the space tourism pilot can concentrate on space boat crews flight training, planning space tourism passenger cargo capacity and preparing space flight manifests , and will as a result, avoid the expense of maintaining a launch operation on a daily basis. In addition, by outsourcing the spacecraft manufacturing, it can avoid spending millions of dollar on facilities and equipment infrastructure and engineering manufacturing expertise.

(3) achieve any space tourism mission plan

On third aspect concerns how to achieve any space tourism mission. Every space tourism mission must be ensure that reliable service is provided to satisfy every space tourism passenger personal space traveler needs and let them to enjoy in their whole space tourism journey, let them to catch a big aircraft in comfortable environment of technologically sophisticated space boat, reasonable and competitive every time space tourism flight ticket price plan is developed and properly revised every time space tourism ticket price when performing their assigned every different space tourism journey mission.

Hence, the space tourism leisure company will provide one careful selected space tourism destination , e.g. Mar planet space tourism journey, Moon planet space tourism journey or no any space destination journey, it means that the space craft only needs to fly one circle around between Earth and Moon space journey etc. that are capable of meeting the requirements of travelling into Earth orbit. So, any space tourism journey must emphasize affordability, reliability, safety, customer service and responsiveness in responding to every client's space tourism journey requirements. Hence, any one of space tourism journey must have clear space journey mission and objective to satisfy any space traveler client target needs.

1.1 Methods to raise space traveler number

Future space tourism will be one kind of new travel leisure market for any new space travel leisure companies to enter this undiscovered market in the beginning. However, how to predict future 10 to 20 years , even more space traveler number that is one important issue to any new space tourism leisure companies.

I think that space tourism leisure companies need to define what kinds of space travel leisure service to be provided to space travelling passengers, however, what age group of space passengers who will be their space travelling target client. For example, their space travel leisure must provide any flight operation that takes one or more passengers beyond the altitude of 100 km and thus into space to let space travelling passengers who have fun, exciting space travelling feeling.

Anyway, for any kind of space tourism (leisure space travel) journey, space tourism leisure company needs anyone to be bring customer satisfaction, it is a plan or predictive methods to measure how to let every space travelling passenger to feel comfortable when they are catching the spacecraft (space flying product) and they can have enjoyable and fun or exciting feeling when they have need providing any space tourism journey, services meet or surpass customer expectations.

Thus, any space tourism leisure company needs to evaluate the degree of every time space tourism journey's customer satisfaction and customer satisfaction is also always evaluated in relationship to the every time ticket price of the space tourism journey. So, the space tourism leisure company will predict the next time of what the space tourism journey of passenger number is more accurate, after it has evaluated what degree of every time space tourism journey's customer satisfaction is. It aims to gather their opinions to find which aspects that they need to revise, e.g. choosing where will be the next time space tourism journey destination, how to improve spacecraft staff's service attitude and performance to serve to their space tourism passengers when they are catching the spacecraft, to evaluate whether the spacecraft can provide comfortable and safe environment to let them to catch in order to let the next time space travelling passengers can feel satisfactory and enjoyable when they are catching the space tourism leisure's spacecraft to fly to anywhere in space.

In general, the expectation of factors space passengers include the following customer value elements, such as below:
● viewing space and the Earth.
● experiencing weightlessness and being able to float freely in zero gravity.
● experiencing pre-flight astronaut training and related sensations.
● communicating from space to significant others.
● being able to discuss the adventure in an informed way.
● having astronaut like documentation and memorabilia.

These objectives need to be combined with, sometimes conflicting constraints, such as guaranteed safe return, limited training time, reasonable comfort, and minimum medical restrictions. All these above issues which will be every space travelling passenger considerate matters before they choose the space tourism leisure company to catch its spacecraft to fly to space. So, all these factors will influence the next time space passenger number. Any space tourism leisure company can not neglect how to solve these all matters before they decide when their next time space tourism journey to be achieved.

Consequently, if the space craft tourism leisure company could revise what aspects of its last space tourism journey to find what are its wrong or weakness or unattractive challenges to cause any one space travelling passenger who feels unsatisfactory. Then, it can have more effort to concentrate on improving its next space tourism journey to raise its space tourism service performance level , e.g. people, food, leisure etc. service aspects and its space tourism product quality level, e.g. proving comfortable spacecraft facilities to let space travelling passengers to catch in whole spacecraft tourism journey. Then, it will have more confidence to achieve the raising space travelling passenger number.

● What is the prediction space travelling passenger desire method ?
The prediction space travelling passenger individual desire method can be one survey investigation method. When every time spacecraft finishes space tourism journey mission, after all space tourism passengers catch the spacecraft to arrive earth from space. When they arrive earth space station destination, then the space tourism leisure company can arrange survey investigation staffs to enquire their feeling for this time space tourism journey immediately.

The survey content can include as below:

Do you feel satisfactory or unsatisfactory to which aspects of this time space tourism journey?

(1) On service aspect questions include as below:

(a) Do you feel space food taste is good?

(b) Do you enjoy this time space tourism journey arrangement?

(c) Do you feel satisfactory to space staff
service performance?

(d) If you have unsatisfactory feeling for any one of above questions, which aspect issue cause you feel unsatisfactory to explain to let us to know in order to us to revise our service performance.

(2) On product aspect questions include as below:

(a) Do you feel comfortable when you are catching our spacecraft in whole space tourism journey?

(b) If you feel comfortable , may you explain the reasons what aspects of our spacecraft has weakness to cause you feel uncomfortable?

(c) Do you feel safe when you are catching our spacecraft in whole space tourism journey?

(d) If you feel unsafe, may you explain the reasons what aspects of our spacecraft has weakness to cause you feel unsafe?

Finally, we thank your ideas to be given to let us know how to improve our every time future space tourism journey in order to find what challenge cause our service performance and product quality which can not satisfy your needs. So, we shall improve to avoid future challenges continue occur. Our mission is achievement of 100% satisfactory level to our every space travelling passenger individual feeling. Also, we hope that you can choose our space tourism leisure service again, when you have another time space tourism leisure desire need. However, we shall revise to improve our service performance and product quality to be better, after collecting your ideas from this time survey investigation. I think you spend time to give your ideas from this survey investigation faithfully.

So, survey investigation method will be one important idea gathering tool to help any space tourism leisure company to revise the weaknesses to raise or improve future every time space tourism journey service performance and product quality to achieve raising competitive effort in this new space tourism leisure market.

Hence, survey investigation method will be the best idea gathering method to predict how space travelling passenger emotion or desire need will change in order to achieve the objective of raising every time space tourism journey future space travelling passenger number more easily for every space tourism leisure company.

● How does price factor won't be the main factor to influence space traveler number when COVID 19 disease brings negative emotion to travellers ?

The space tourism leisure organizations indicate the total cost of a trip into space is rapidly coming down from the initial price level of about US$600,000, it is obvious that the space travelling customer base is going to be rather small. Typical customers tend to belong to the top 1% income bracket. They also indicate that the price comes down , it is expected that new space travelling customer groups will enter the space tourism leisure market.

Typical new customers include people in other brackets with one-of-a kind incomes, such as inheritance or business sold. There are indications that those types of customers are becoming interested in spending on an once-in-a lifetime space experience. Therefore, the growth of the space tourism market is highly sensitive to customer satisfaction and how it is communicated through various media.

This will establish the status factors of space tourism and corresponding brand reputation service providers. They also suggest that any operator monitors space travelling customer satisfaction closely, as it will help developing increasingly accurate estimates of how the space tourism leisure market will develop.

Hence, it seems that every time space tourism journey price variable factor will influence the time space tourism of customer individual leisure desire and the space tourism passenger number. For example, the minimum price goal foe a variable space tourism business is currently estimate to be below

US$3000-4000/kg for a round -trip depending on variable configuration and operation size. At this price, they estimate that somewhat over 1 % of the high income earners are potential customers.

However, for significant volume growth the longer term goal should be below US$2000/kg for a typical passenger, baggage and supplies. The lower price will probably open space tourism to a broader population, expanding the customer base and altering expectations. beyond this point space tourism will become into a travelling competitive leisure commodity, price competition will ensure and service providers need to rethink their space tourism marketing and branding and price strategies.

I shall also recommend how to attract the potential customers successfully. First, space operators need to pay special attention to the right level of customer services. Second, various preparatory customer operations cost, such as a travel to the launch site, space tourism destination accommodation, pre-flight training, medical check-ups and equipment my add up to between 10 to 15 % of the actual space travel cost. Thurs, solving the right balance between services offered and cost of client operation in order to earn the largest intangible benefits, such as loyalty, confidence, leisure enjoyment, comfortable space travelling journey as well as tangible benefits, such as profit, spacecraft manufacturing facilities, space stations, space hotels , space swimming pools, space gardens, space cinema etc. which are built to similar to earth building facilities to satisfy space travelers' needs.

1.2 The influential factors persuade travelers choose space tourism

Nowadays, our earth is no longer an adventurous enough place for some experienced tourists. Space tourism will be a new sector of adventure tourism, which is in the near future will be fast becoming a new tourism leisure opportunity for experiencing the unknown. Of one day, space tourism is able to reach the mass tourism phase, due to improved safety and decreased operation costs, a future space tourist will possibly only need minimal training to cope with the zero cost.

Space tourism is quite well established with visits to space attraction and launch sites, and it is a wealthy trips to the international space station for any space tourism travelers. However, if any space tourism leisure companies can attempt to find what the most influential factors are to persuade travelers feel attraction more than travelling in our earth.

It aims to let travelers to choose space travelling more than earth travelling when they feel travelling leisure need. I shall indicate what will be the most important influential factors to persuade travelers to choose space tourism more than earth tourism as below:

Firstly, I shall argue that the majority of different new space tourism journey destinations will be needed to find to satisfy different aged space travelers and different income space tourism consumers' needs. For example, the rich people have effort to consume longer time and reach any space tourism destinations where are far away from our earth of their every space tourism journey.

Otherwise, the middle income people will choose shorter space tourism journey distance from our earth and short time space tourism journey. Also, younger space tourism clients can accept more longer journey time, exciting fast speed spacecraft flying journey. Otherwise, old space tourism clients can only accept comfortable and shorter time safe space journey. So, it seems that safety, comfortable feeling, shorter time space tourism journey won't be one important influential factor to excite any young people who choose to consume space tourism leisure. Otherwise, safety, comfortable feeling, shorter time space tourism journey will be one important influential factor to excite any old people who choose to consume space tourism leisure.

Secondly, the another most important influential factor to excite space travelers to choose space tourism , it concerns whether the space travelers will feel what tourists benefits can be earned from a substantial variety of destinations choice. In general, space tourism with those of aviation, space travelers will hope space tourism will be travelling distances by air in a very short time, safely and comfortably, to bring them to arrive any space planet destinations when spacecraft reaches any space stations to stay in any space destinations.

Hence, space destination factor will bring important influential choice to any space destination journeys. As a result of the space technological tourism boom, the number of potential different space destination, choice attractions have grown with far fewer places on earth to which human do have access yet. However, the ultimate different space destinations to which many of us dream is not on earth, but as least 100 km above us, anywhere in space any planets.

If the space tourism leisure company can provide different space tourism destination choices to young or old age both space traveler target consumer groups. They will feel a real holiday when they will be able to enjoy a great image of the earth from planets. It might mean that every space tourism journey can provide different space tourism destination to let space travelers have another new travelling destinations where are far from our earth anywhere.

Hence, the different space tourism destinations will give them an unforgettable adventure. Think of how it would be to be able to check in at a " billion strategy" luxury hotel in space one planet, it means that the space planet destination can provide one luxury hotel to let space travelers to live one night or more in the space planet destination, how it would be to schedule the space traveler' vacation at one of the space tourism leisure company luxury resorts on the Moon or Mars.

This images seem from science fiction movies, but one should not forget that 100 years ago, the Wright brothers, aviation pioneers inventors and builders of the air plane, would not have imagined how, every day it is possible that future spacecraft can fly to any planets to let human have chance to stay in the space hotel one night or more.

Consequently, space destination choice and space tourism journey service performance, aviation safety, ticket price and leisure satisfactory feeling which will be important influential factors to attract future space travelers to choose space tourism leisure to replace earth tourism leisure in future one day.

1.3 Raising space tourism leisure
consumption strategies

Although, space tourism industry is a real enjoyment and exciting travelling leisure to human. It is possible that human will choose to consume space tourism leisure to replace earth tourism leisure, if human felt that earth tourism leisure is not attractive to them to consume to go to anywhere to travel in their leisure time.

But, I believe that space tourism industry has still many factors to influence human to choose to consume space tourism leisure, even they will consider space tourism leisure consumption I is only one time space tourism in their life time. Hence, space tourism companies ought achieve this aim to persuade or attract everyone prefer to spend space tourism leisure at least one time in their life, then it can represent success. However, I think to achieve this aim, it has these challenges to influence their success, even they believe space tourism leisure business is one potential attractive travel entertainment business. These challenges include such as: expensive space tourism ticket price issue, catching spacecraft safe issue, space traveler personal body health issue, age issue, family and friend relationship influence issue, working time and holiday time arrangement issue, the space trip arrangement issue, weather issue etc. different challenges, which will have possible to influence every space tourism planner either who decide change to cancel the time space tourism plan, or forgive to choose space tourism leisure in their life forever.

Hence, how to raise space tourism leisure consumption desire will be one considerable matter for any space tourism leisure businessmen. I shall indicate my personal three aspect of strategical opinions to let them to know how to raise every space tourism planner individual space tourism leisure consumption desire to avoid every time space tourism passenger number will have decrease failure chance as below:

● (1) Strategic opinion

On the first aspect of strategic opinion, I feel that the space education tutor can teach new space knowledge to let every space traveler to learn any new space and earth knowledge during he/she is catching on the spacecraft in personal contact learning experience environment which can raise space tourism consumption desire. The reason is because the space tourism leisure traveler can raise extra space and earth learning knowledge when they can catch the spacecraft to fly and contact the space environment to learn and feel what the differences are between space and earth by himself or herself. Hence, it is very attractive to the space traveler student target group and I believe that their parents will encourage their sons or daughters to participate the time of space trip and they are more preferable to help them to buy the time space trip ticket, due to their sons and daughters can learn any space knowledge when they are studying. Moreover, every space traveler will feel surprise to learn any new space and earth knowledge from the space tutor's teaching, due to he/she is unknown that this space travel trip includes learning space and earth knowledge.

I suggest that the space tourism leisure businessmen can give learning opportunity to every travel trip space travelers to feel that this space actual environment can bring what disadvantages or advantages to influence our earth when they are catching aircraft to fly to space to travel in every space trip. The space and earth learning knowledge can include these two aspects of space learning knowledge and experience below:

On the teaching of space environment learning knowledge hand, the topics can include as below:

Firstly the space learning topic can concern how space environment influences water and hydrated minerals change , they can learn what our drinking water function how is applied to space environment. For example, in the space environment, they can learn and attempt to feel that how water can be used in protecting astronauts against harmful radiation from the sun and cosmic rays by cloaking spacecraft with a thin layer of water in the actual space environment as well as the space travelers can also feel water is same as fuel when they are catching the spacecraft, they can feel the water is heavy to transport into space when they are catching the spacecraft to fly to space during their whole space tourism journey.

Moreover, when their spacecraft reaches anyone of planets and it stays on the planet's space station, e.g. Moon space station. They can learn how to attempt to contact the hydrated minerals to learn and feel what they contained in some asteroids may be possible sources of water and fuel in the actual space environment. When they are walking in actual space environment, such as Moon planet, they can contact or touch this hydrated minerals to learn how water molecules can be extracted and separated chemically to produce hydrogen fuel knowledge in the actual space environment. This is one exciting space learning experience to the space travelling student passengers.

Secondly the space learning topic can concern how human fights space threats , even when their whole space leisure journey, the space science teacher can let the space trip student passengers to feel that they are learning new space knowledge between the space science teacher and whose space trip student passengers. Such as how to protect our earth knowledge: Teaching them to know when will be threats to our earth from space. The space science teacher can explain how this space threating environment influences our life safety and let them to feel that a mass extinction can be triggered if an asteroid 10 kilometers across hit the earth. Even being the apex species in the food chain did not space carnivorous dinosaurs from such disaster, who knows if this terrifying scene won't happen before our eyes? So, the space travelers can image and feel how the space threating environment can influence their life safety in the actual space environment as well as the space science teacher can let whose space travelers to feel and image the actual earth disaster will possible happen suddenly to let they feel afraid in the actual space environment. Also the space science teacher can teach how our earth can fright the space stones attack to let the space traveler to know, when an impactor targets an asteroid for a controlled well-times wallop. The collision will change the asteroid's momentum, deflecting it from its original orbital path which intersects with that of the earth. So, at the moment, the space travelers can image they are a larger spacecraft near an asteroid which can also change the path. Given enough time, the gravitational pull from the spacecraft will be able to steer the asteroid away from the earth. So, every space traveler will feel that they are catching the spacecraft in the safe space environment to avoid the Earth disaster from space sudden unpredictable attack.

It is more fun real space tourism knowledge learning feel to let every space traveler has chance to learn any new space science knowledge when he/she is catching the spacecraft to fly to space to travel. Hence, one successful space trip ought include trip and learning experience both contents in order to raise every the space tourism planner individual space trip consumption desire.

● (2) Strategic opinion

On the second aspect of strategic opinion, space tourism leisure companies need to let planning travelers feel that anyone of space tourism leisure is very different to general tourism leisure. In general, tourism leisure is visiting at least one night for leisure and holiday, business or other tourism purposes in Earth only. Otherwise, space tourism leisure is other kind of an unique trip leisure or entertainment method, e.g. the space traveler can catch the spacecraft to visit any planets to stay to live at the planet's space hotel at least one night, e.g. Future potential populated Moon or Mars space hotel space trip. Moreover, the space travel companies ought give chance to let them to feel what weightless feeling is in weightlessness environment when they are walking on Moon or other planets in possible. Even, they can attempt to build these entertainment facilities, instead of space hotels, such as space swimming pools, space gardens, space cinema etc. building facilities. It aims to let them to feel what the differences between Earth and space life when they are walking on the Moon, when they are swimming on the space pools, when they are living in space hotels, when they are watching movies in space cinemas, when they are seeing flowers and different species of planets and fruits. e.g. oranges, apples, bananas, and vegetable and potatoes and tomatoes in space gardens. It is very exciting and fun space trip life experience between one days to seven days. So, they believe that they must not feel these space life experience if they do not choose to participate this time space trip planning journey by the space trip company preparation.

Also, due to that the space tourism passengers need to the pre-flight checks and training before they ensure to qualify to permit to participate the space trip. So space travel companies need to concern how to take care their health check and training matter considerately. It aims to let every space traveler will feel a market segment with fitness and extreme experiences as well as he/she will become popular with a market segment passenger to the space tourism leisure company, although he/she must not guarantee to pass the space training and/or pre-flight health checks to permit to participate the space trip. However, he/she can believe that he/she is one worth space travelling passenger to the space tourism leisure company, even this time pre-flight health check or/and the short time space trip training requirements are failure. However, the space tourism leisure company must need to let all pre-flight health check and space trip training passengers to feel that it is only one space tourism which can give them and let customers view the space travel is as the ultimate showcase for health, even though a majority of the population can pass the pre-flight medical and other tests in order to raise their confidence and safety to catch the spacecraft to fly to space to travel when they are confirmed to pass these tests to permit to catch the spacecraft later.

In general, the expectations of future space passengers include the following customer value elements, such as below:

● Viewing space and the Earth.

● Experiencing weightlessness and experiencing pre-flight astronaut training and related sensations.

● Communicating from space to significant others.

● Being able to discuss the adventure in an informed way.

● Having astronaut-like documentation and memorabilia.

● Enjoying one exciting and fun space trip.

However, instead of considering these objectives need to be combined with, sometimes conflicting , constraints such as guaranteed safe, return , limited training time, reasonable comfort, and minimum medical restrictions. So, space tourism companies need to reduce every space traveler individual worries before they decide to make the time of space tourism journey. Then, it can increase their confidence to raise their space tourism consumption desire more successfully.

Consequently, instead of these consideration, a space travel operator must pay attention to the total customer experience over the entire customer process, starting from how the service is presented, proposed and sold. The service package must include training, instructions, travel to the launch site and various post. Travel activities to generate maximum customer satisfaction and brand building opportunity.

● (3) Strategic opinion

On the final aspect of strategic opinion, I think any space tourism companies space tourism companies need to consider every time space tourism ticket price and space tourism trip issues. It is important factor to influence every space traveler individual consumption desire. Due to space trip ticket price must be more expensive to compare common Earth trip travelling ticket price, so this kind of tourism leisure market target customer will be the rich and high income customer group.

On the space trip ticket challenge issue, despite that fact the total cost of a trip into space is rapidly coming down from the initial price level of about US$60,000, it is obvious that the customer base is going to be rather small and the client target customer is only high income or rich consumer group. Typical customers tend to belong to the top of the top 1% income bracket. So, ensures that space traveler number must be less than common Earth traveler number.

Also, such as the space trip ticket price, it is expected that new middle rich level or middle high level income customer target group will enter the space trip leisure market, when every space trip ticket price falls down about 1% Typical new customers include people in other income brackets with one-of-a-kind incomes, such as inheritance or business sold space traveler target group. These people will be space travel new client group, when its every space trip ticket price can be reduced to close 1 to 2 % nearly. If any space tourism leisure companies expect to attract new rich and/or high income target customer group to choose any one kind of space trip journey planning to consume.

These are indications that these types of customers are becoming interested in spending on an once-in-a-lifetime space experience. Therefore, the growth of the space tourism market is highly sensitive to customer satisfaction and how it is communicated through the various media. This will establish the status –factor of space tourism, and corresponding brand reputation of service providers. The minimum price goal for a variable space tourism business is currently estimate to be below US$3-4000/kg for a round-trip depending on vehicle configuration. So, space travel leisure companies need to concern every round space trip cost, it can depend on the space vehicle number and weight issue to influence every space trip ticket price variable to achieve how much it can earn.

On space journey design factor aspect, it includes these different facilities aspects how to design, because future space travelling consumers will concern whether the space travel company can provide special entertainment to satisfy their needs. The facilities include as below:

How to design space hotels to let them to live in comfortable space environment and eat the best taste and fresh food quality when the cookers need to cook in the space hotel in the space environment? How to design space swimming pools to let them to swim in safe space environment? How to design space sport centers to let them to run more easily in one space sport warm and safe environment? How to design one space garden to let them to see different species of Earth flowers, or plants? How to design one space farming land to let them to see different species of Earth fruits, vegetables, tomatoes, potatoes etc. fresh foods growth in warm and safe space farming land environment? How to design one space cinema to let them to watch movies in one safe and warm space cinema environment? All these facilities will be any one of future space trip's' important and attractive space trip leisure facilities to influence every space traveler to choose to buy the space tourism leisure company's space trip leisure service.

Instead of these space building entertainment facilities, they also need to concern how the space vehicle entertainment tools are provided the entertainment service to satisfy their needs. When the space travelers can sit on the space vehicles to move on any planets' lands, such as Moon. A number of space vehicle options exist in the market, mainly differing based on the seat capacity as well as the in-flight experience level offered. The typical space vehicle solution is a small, relatively light weight spacecraft taking between 2 to 10 passengers. The number of passengers depends on the service level, amenities and extra offered. The trip typically lasts about 10 hours and of which about 4 hours are spent in space. The main attraction is the weightless time after in space. The main attraction is the weightless time after re-entry has started. It is a rather low-G technology and therefore the medical requirements for participants are nor very high.

Consequently, the space vehicles, space leisure building facilities, the space trip reasonable price ticket level, every safe space trip journey arrangement, clean and fresh and good taste space food arrangement, space traveler individual real learning experience etc. these factors will be the main influential factors to raise the space tourism leisure company's competitive effort and the space traveler consumer individual consumption desire to the space tourism leisure company in the future.

Can COVID 19 disease influence Space travel marketing strategy changes?

Any space travel organization needs have good marketing strategy to prepare how to operate its space travelling leisure business in order to attract many space travelling clients to choose its space travelling service. I shall indicate these different strategies aspects whey they are needed to be concerned as below:

2.1 On concept of spacecraft design aspect

Firstly, on concept aspect, any one space travelling leisure company needs have at least one spacecraft to catch clients to fly to space to travel. So how to design the spacecraft and its quality and safety and comfortable environment spacecraft machine concept aspect issue which is one challenge to be concerned. Because many space travelling passengers ususally concern whether the spacecraft is safe, comfortable , good quality, as well as the space travelling leisure providers also need to concern whether the spacecraft is less time and energy saving efficient use, less manufactory operating cost and durable.

In general, space travelling leisure provider expects the spacecraft or spacecraft vehicle can be uesed long time. The spacecraft will be expected to utilize previous flight rated and proven technologies to from the basis for manufacturing spacecraft vehicles , and will incorporate the latest modern avionics and flight system for answering safety, reliability and economical operation.

In general, the spacecraft will be designed to carry two crew and approximately, 10,000 pounds of cargo, depending on the ultimate weight of the spacecraft. Relying on flight hardware to maintain the space station, such as Moon or Mar space station is fpr any space travelling spacecrafts to reach these space travelling destinations to stay, it is also need to consider by many space travelling experts as risky, extremely, expensive cost sensitive for any space station travelling destination design arrangement in order to future every spacecraft can fly to any planets to stay on its space station safely.

(1) Outsourcing spacecraft concept design strategy

As a result, outsourcing strategy is one good method to help them to reduce cost in order to achieve to let every space travel passenger has safe space journey experience and capacity for safely launching a fully loaded

(including crew and cargo). Outsourcing strategy is the launch role to a major contracor, they can concentrate on crew flight training, planning all passnegers and cargo capacoty, and preparing flight manifests, and will as a result, avoid the expense of maintaining a launch operation on a daily basis. In addition, by outsoucing the spacecraft manufacturing, the space travelling provider can avoid spending millions of dollars on facilities and equipment infrastructure and engineering manufacturing expertise.

(2) On deciding misson aspect

Secondly, on mission aspect, any space travelling journey needs have a clear mission to be planned how to achieve in order to ensure every space travelling passenger feel satisfactory in the space travelling journey. So, every whole space travelling journey arrangement, e.g. where will be the space travelling destination, how to check every space travelling planned passengers' bodies whether who are health to catch spacecraft to fly to space to travel or how to train every space travelling planned passenger to ensure whom can permit to catch spacecraft to fly to space to travel, how to arrange every space travelling journey entertainment and facilities to let either young or old age target passenger to enjoy the space trip to feel satisfactory, how to arrange different days of every space trip.
In the last few years, Virgin Galactic has been making new's headlines with its promises to provide space travel services, and announcement that it will soom offer, at quite a hefty price, trips to sub-orbit. It is generally agreed that sub-orbit exists 100 kilometres above the earth's sea-level (Von Der Dunk, 2012). Hence, Virgin Galactic will provide travel to where customers may experience weightlessness, as well as the sight of earth's curvature. Even more interesting is that Virgin Galactic is not the only company with such a mission,there are a few more that wish to offer the same type of service. For example, some companies even aim to provide an orbital type of flight.
Orbit flight suggests that humans would venture into outer space, where they might either orbit the earth or board the international space station (hereinafter: ISS). In addition, some envision space hotels, moon visitations and mining asteroids. Although at first such statement might seem for one must point out that a "space hotel" is already in earth's orbit and that diligent progress through flight tests is almost made the commercial aspect of regular space travel a reality; it is only the question of time and readiness for the companies to make their long-awaited and open a new industry of

present day economics (Klemm & Markkanen, 2011; Berry , 2012).

So, every space travelling mission is to ensure that reliable, technologically-sophisicated competitively-priced flight certified spacecraft are designed and properly maintained when performing their every assigned space travelling journey mission. The space traveller leisure provider will need to provide a carefully selected array of techologies that are capable of meeting the requirements of travelling into earth orbit. It will emphasize affordability, reliability, safety, customer service and responsiveness in responding to customer's space travelling requirements.

For this space tourism leisure mission example, it many include these objectives , such as below:

One trip into space, sending a space vehicle of a certain make and with a specify capacity on a space mission, provides the various grades of a core service, such as a space mission including issues such as waiting and delivery times, personal attention and advice, amenities and facilities, ensure quality assurance, it is the planned and system activities implemented in a quality system. So that quality requirements for a product or service will be fulfilled. It aims at preventing high-risk adverse events, or reducing thei impact, provides excellent customer satisfaction, it is a measure of how products and services meet the space travelling customer expectations, customer satisfaction is also always evaluated in relationship of every space travelling ticket price of the space travelling entertainment service and spacecraft product comfortable environment feeling and good leisure arrangement for every space travelling leisure journey.

(3) On space tourism leisure organization managment aspect

Thirdly, on space tourism leisure organization management aspect, it is also important to influence efficient and excellent space service performance to be provided to satisfy every space travel organization management team needs to be consists of experienced professionals who have successfully management and operated companies specializing in the aerospace industry for a number of years.

Their knowledge and contacts within the space industry will prove invaluable in assisting the space tourism leisure provider in the achievement of its goals and objectives. In individuals on the team components that up a spacecraft tourism development organization, and have unique experience in the design, construction, operations and maintenance of the major functions will developing spacecraft for launching into orbit. Every spacecraft will be built and maintained utilizing the same high standards of quality, within budget and well within time constraints.

Hence, every space tourism provider needs have one excellent management leaders to manage every space tourism service staffs to serve passengers in order to achieve excellent service performance to let them every one to feel satisfactory, during their every space tourism journey (trip).

(4) On target audience prediction aspect

On target audience prediction aspect, every space trip needs have identifies target travelling passenger in order to concentrate to choose the most popular and satisfactory space travelling journey for their identified needs.

For primary audiences example, it can include space enthusiasts and educational families both. Space enthusiasts target are usually young people and they are only 20% over 65 age old people target space ethusiasts who will be the future potential space tourism target consumers as well as the educational families target who will aspect owning educational experience for children , who is the explicit reason to visit space, either he/she has interest in history of space exploration or he/she has interest in future of space exploration or he/she feels that spce trip looked like fun.

KSCVC Visots (2013) indicated that future top markets, ranked by high visitation against space enthusiasts and educational families space tourism passengers, the US cities will include: Orlando, NYC, Miami, Tampa Bay, Chicago, West plam, Philadelphia, Atlanta, Boston, Washington, DC and San Francisco cities. So, future US space travelling market will be the top one in the world.

(5) On space objective aspect

On space objective aspect, instead of any one space tourism leisure organization concerns how to achieve its mission to satisfy all space tourism passengers leisure needs. Although, it is the major missin for space tourism leisure industry. But they can not neglect what the objectives are in order to develop or achieve long term space tourism leisure missions more easily.

The objectives main open space key issues can include such as: Providing an adequate supply of land to meet the future needs of strategic opn space links, natural areas and recreational facilities on any future space tourism destinations, increasing pressure for public access to open space areas with conservation values, competing interests between adjoining land use and development on public open space and its user groups, use of public open space and recreational resources for drainage purposes, raising higher space traveller hotel residential development placing increased pressure on the demand for public open space planet land use aim and developing public open space mor intensive leisure and sport activities on any future new space tourism planet destinations.

When the space tourism leisure providers have long term objectives to attempt to solve above these any one of key issues. It will ahve a more clear objective to achieve its long term space tourism leisure business market. It's long term objectives can include such as below:

To identify existing and future active and passive recreation needs and social trends of future space tourism visitors; to provide a wide range of high quality and accessible public open space public land areas to encourage physical activity and social interaction to meet the existing and future needs of space travelling visitors; to identify existing gaps in the public open space network and develop any different kinds of space trip arrangement to satisfy the different identified target space traveller individual needs; to protect enhance and increase landcrapt values of public open space land use; to recognize the hierarchy of public open space assets; equitably distributing open space resources; access to facilities and a diverse range of opportunities to incorporate the drainage function in public open space travelling destination areas without detriment to safely, environmental, visual and recreational values.

So, these development of any space planets howo to use their lands objectives will bring long term space travelling destination beneficial advantages to raise to build the space hotels, space swimming pools, space gardens, space cinemas, space sport places to let future space travelers can stay in Mars or Moon planet destinations to enjoy these leisure facilities and they can feel which are similar to our earth leisure facilities attractively.

These space buildings are important to attract future space travellers to catch spacecraft to fly to Mars or Moon planet to travel in possible because it is fun and exciting space trip when these leisure facilities can be built on Moon or Mars to let space travellers to stay short days in either these two planets to live their space hotels. So how to build any one of these space leisure building which is another important objective for any future space tourism leisure business, instead of how to arrange any space destination trip objective. So, any space tourism leisure provider ought not neglect how to achieve these two main space tourism objectives.

However, these are key questions continually asked regarding the viability of space tourism. They concern financial, marketing and political communities. Their concerns can be best addredded in a properly, comprehensive business plan. Some questions can not be answered definitively at this time. Hoever, knowledge of the concerns and developing space businesses in any space traveling leisure planning stages and efforts to raise capital in the following questions, every spce tourism leisure business leader needs to concern this questions as below:

Can the space tourism industry into a profitable enonomic industry?

Are challenges related to financing, marketing, business methodologies or a combination of all of these facets?

Can the proponents of space tourism to be proven business tools and methodologies in their presentation of an acceptable business plan?

Can at least a cost effective, certified passenger space tourism journey to be developed for space tourism?

What effects will influence space-tourism businesses of NASA begins selling seats on the US space shuttle to civilian space tourists?

All above questions will be every new space tourism leisure businessman who needs to concern questions in order to achieve whose marketing strategy more successfully. Consequently, marketing strategy is important to be prepared in order to follow corrective steps to achieve every space tourism leisure business missions and objectives more easily.

2.2 Space tourism leisure behavioral economic consumption model

In space tourism leisure industry, due to every time space trip needs the space travelling planner to plan how much budget to consume expensive spce ticket price. So, it seems that the target customers will be rich or high income level young people or the retirement rich old people target customer group.

So, it brings this question: How to persuade these rich or high income young people or rich retirement old people to prefer to spend spce tourism leisure at least one time in their life?

It is one valuabe research question to every future space tourism leisure provider. I shall indicate the successful factors to analyze how to persuade them to accept this kind of potential space travelling leisure in behavioral economic personal consumption view point, in order to explain the cause and effect relationship between of these factors as below:

(1) Economic environment variable factor

Firstly, it is economic environment variable factor whether it can influence to space tourism leisure consumption changing. As I discuss about economic environment variable issue will influence consumption behavior changing. For space tourism leisure case, it is not now kind of essential consumption leisure product to every one. So , even the rich or high income people who will be influences to seek this kind of leisure to play, it the economic environment is improved, it will influence they have positive attitude and interest to choose this kind of leisure consumption. However, if the economic environment is worse, it will influence they have negative attitude and no interest to choose this kind of leisure consumption, due to space travel is one kind of expensive leisure consumption to every one.

Hence, in this space tourism leisure industry, it does not ensure that the rich or high income people must be persuade to choose this kind of expensive space tourism entertainment in whose holiday or retirement time. They can have the common tourism entertainment to go to different countries to travel many times in our earth. Otherwise, space tourism leisure is more expensive to compare common earth tourism leisure , it means that the rich or high income people only spend one time spacecraft catching to fly to space to travel in their life, it is more difficult to every space traveler like to catch spacecraft to fly to space to travel more than one time, due to he/she had attempted to catch spacecraft to fly to space to travel to own space travel experience, he/she will feel enough satisfactory and enjoyment in common. Hence, it is possible that future many rich or high income people only like to spend one time space tourism leisure, then they won't continue to spend this kind of tourism entertainment again in their life.

Thus, space tourism leisure providers need to arrange any special or attractive space tourism leisure to persuade these high income or rich target clients to consume, when the economic environment will change worse. The Europen space agency (ESA), defines this phenomenon between economic environment variable and space tourism client growth or falling number relationship as: " space tourism is an execution of sub-orbital flight by privately finded and/or privately operated vehicles and the technology development driven by space tourism market."

it seems that space vehicle is one attractive travelling desire tool will be one attractive selling point to influence space tourism leisure consumer individual entertainment choice or attitude to be changed to positive leisure consumption attitude to prefer to play this kind of space tourism activities when economic environment changes to worse. Hence, when economic environment is worse, the economic wore changing factor will influence the space travelling planner individual leisure consumption desire, even it will influence the rich or high income young people or rich retirement people target customer both groups.

As (ESA, 2008) indicated space vehicle will be one kind of attractive leisure tool for spce traveler. So, I suggest that space tourism lesiure journey arrangement needs to include that such as : the space travelers can catch space vehicle to move on Moon or Mars plants land to feel what the different feeling is between during they are catching public transportation tool, such as bus or taxi during the are catching these transportation tools on earth land and during they are catching space vehicle tools on Mars or Moon planet's lands. It is so exciting and fun catching space vehicle tool experience on these both Mars or Moon planets' lands to the young and old age space travelling passengers. Because every space vehicle's speed is not very fast and it will move on Moon or Mars planets slowly. So, any aged pace travelling passengers can attempt to play this kind of space facilities leisure after they catched spacecraft to fly to these both Mars or Moon planet to stay. They can spend half hour or one hour, even more than one hour to catch the space vehicle to go to anywhere on Mars or Moon to travel. It is possible that they can find exciting and undiscovered things on these both planets.

So, catching space vehicle to go to anywhere on either these both planets journey, it will one essential part of space travelling journey during the economic environment is changed to worse. It is extra attractive space travelling leisure journey to attract space tourism consumer individual leisure desire when economic environment is worse.

Hence, from this perspective then space tourism could be understood as a section of the tourism industry mainly based on technological development, progression and its activitity being related specifically to sub orbital flights. So, if future space tourism providers expect whether the global economic environment changing will be better or worse which won't influence space tourism leisure consumption desire to be changed. The space tourism leisure providers need to persuade the space tourism planners feel space tourism would have to be treated like an already exciting part of the tourism industry. It means that space tourism leisure is one kind of tourism leisure choice to replace common earth tourism leisure consumption. When travelers feel space tourism is another tourism leisure to replace which can replace common earth tourism leisure. It will avoid the worse economic environment changing factor to reduce the rich or high income young people or rich retirement old people whose space travelling leisure consumption desire.

Consequently , the question in relation to, in what kinds of space tourism journey message do space travel providers promote behind whether space vehicle journey promotion message which is needed when economic environment will change worse. I shall be asked, as understanding the meaning in which space tourism is being marketed, communicated is seen as a factor , which can either positively contribute to future development of the tourism industry or lead into prolonging or seen stopping the space tourism industry from its progression.

(2) Space tourism leisure journey management factor

Secondly, space tourism leisure jounrey management factor, how to arrange every space tourism leisure journey which will be one important factor to influence space tourism planner individual tourism consumption desire.

In general, it can includes these several forms of space tourism leisure activities in every space lesiure trip arrangement. The following classification of space tourism include: Terrestria spce tourism (i.e. NASA visit centre, space movies, online space experience); Atmospheric space tourism (i.e. : MIG 31 flight, zero G. flights) and astro (orbita) tourism (i.e.: trips to the international space station-beyond earth orbit) (Cater 2010, Crouch et al. 2009).

Instead of US domestic space tourism market is potential, next country is Japan. First, the study is made by Collins et. al (1994, 1996) in Japan on 3030 research participants, showed that 80% of respondents under the age of 50 were willing to travel to space and out of them 20% were willing to pay year's salary for the space travel experience. Yet, it could be citicized that the Japan people age group of under 50 could be too broad, in general different generations under one groups. nest besides the willingness to go to space, the Japanese study showed respondents motivations for travelling to space, including any fun and exciting attractive space tourism journey, e.g. interest in space walk, catching space vehicle or driving space vehicle on the either Moon or Mars planets, earth view, zeo gravity experience, livin gin space hotels one night or more, watching movies in space cinemas, swimming in space pools, visiting space gardens, running in space sport centers, catching spacecrafts to view earth or Moon or Mars planets.

Hence, it seems attractive space tourism journey can persuade another country's space travelling planners, such as Japanese attempts to satisfy whose space tourism needs. So, different kinds of attractive space trip journey arrangement will be one important factor to influence young and old age travelling consumption desire. It implies that attractive space tourism journey will be one influential factor to encourage other countries tourism consumers attempt to another kind of leaving earth tourism leisure. So, any space tourism trip destinations and leisure facilities arrangement must need to satisfy space traveler individual leisure needs and every space trip must be more fun, exciting and comfortable and enjoyable feeling to compare general tourism journey in earth. Due to general earth tourism leisure will be space tourism leisure's competitive or replaced leisure product and service. Hence, space trip destinations and leisure facilities choice will be one important factor to influence space travelling planner's consumption desire.

Every space travelling planner will compare general earth travelling leisure's destinations and leisure facilities arrangement whether the space travelling trip arrangement , leisure facilities arrangement and food arrangement, space vehicle or spacecraf leisure comfortable influence issues which will have more satisfactory enjoyable feeling to compare general earth tourism leisure and their spending expenditure to every space trip whether is value or is not value.

Consequently, economic environment changing factor and space trip and leisure facilities arrangement factor which both will influence any space tourism planner individual consumption desire mainly. So, space tourism businessmen ought concern these two aspects of factors how and when will change to adapt any country's potential space traveler's space tourism changing taste and needs in order to follow the new space tourism changing needs easily.

Space tourism market moral ethic risk
threats

What are space tourism moral ethic risk during the space businessmen operate this businesses as well as what market threats who will encounter to face difficulties ? I shall give actul cases to explain how and why these challenges will cause to influence any new space tourism businesses development successfully.

(1) Potential accidents aspect
Firstly, space travelers will concern that public reactions to potential accidents aspect during they are catching spacecrafts to travel to space. In

fact, it is moral ethic responsibility to any space tourism leisure providers to provide safe, comfortable and non accident occurrence in their whole space trip. Because once time accident will cause any one of space passenger hurt or death. So , it must be any space tourism businessmen responsibilities to concern whether they have enough confidence to ensure none any accident occurrences in every space tourism trip.

Hence, in space tourism industry, government needs have public policy to threaten or prohibit any space tourism leisure providers neglect to often check and ensure any spacecraft machines or equipments are regular opeations, as well as often renew new spacecraft machines when they are old to be used. The policy is a force effort to need them to abide every space tourism leisure safe responsibility to ensure or guarantee any one of spacecraft won't have accident occurrences during it has left earth to fly to space in whole space trip journey from the beginning to the end till to the spacecraft come to earth safely.

Hence, this policy forces any space tourism leisure providers concern to put a monetary value on increased or reduced risk of death, the " value of statistical live", used to characterize when the benefit of safety regulation is worth the cost such regulation improves. So, the country government and the country's space tourism leisure providers both have responsibilities to guarantee all space tourism passengers' life safety. It must not allow any death or hurt occurrences during every space tourism trip.

Even, the country government can have legal action to publish any space tourism leisure providers, when their every space tourism trip has occurred accidents, e.g. fire accident occurrence in spacecarft or spacecrat machines are broken to be damaged and need to be repaired during the space tourism trip. It will threaten to reduce trip accident occurrence, such as this cases. The commercial space ventures may present risk to property as well, such as a fire starting on the ground by launch-related material or problems presented by space debris.

In principle, liability law can provide incentive to deter carelessness that could lead to the destruction of property, although statutory (rather than common law) assignments of liability for commercial launches are somewhat problematic.

Consequently, if the space tourism leisure provider expected to grow space tourism passenger number in long -term time, it must need to ensure none any accidents can occur during any space trip. Otherwise, the space tourism passengers can choose another space tourism leisure provider to replace its spce tourism leisure easily.

(2) Space tourism destinations and space tourism entertainment facilities safe arrangement challenges aspect

Secondly, it is space tourism destinations and space tourism entertainment facilities safe arrangement challenges. Nowadays, commercial space travel is looking more like a real possibility than science fiction. The usual ethical issues related to the safety of the space destination choices and the space tourism entertainment facilities, e.g. space vehicles, space hotels, space swimming pools, space sport centers, space cinemas, space gardens, space farming lands. In this strange space environment and safety concerns are just the beginning as there are othe interesting questions, such as below:

What likely would be a fair process for commercializing or claiming property in any space planets? Such as Moon or mars, when any future space tourism leisure providers who need to build above these any one of space entertainment facilities on these planets to provide to their space travelling customers to play.

How to distribute and manage these any lands ownership to these future space tourism providers fairly and legally?

How likely would a separatist movement be among space settlements to want to be free and independent states?

How to ensure above future space entertainment facilities and space entertainment places are in the safe space environment to be provided to any space travelers to play in any planets, e.g. Moon or Mars etc. planets.

So, concerning how to arrange space entertainment facilities to provide to space tourism clients to play in any safe space environment issue, it will be another concerning question to every space tourism leisure providers. When they decide to choose anywhere to the space hotels, space swimming pools, space gardens, space cinemas or space farming lands or space sport centers. These space buildings will need to be built in the safe, on stable stone lands environment and none any natural distaster, such as large wind or space underground water etc. unpredictable space natural distasterr attack to these space buildings suddenly. Because it has responsibility to any space tourism leisure providers to guarantee any one of these space buildings are safe to be built in the planet's safe land environment. It aims to achieve none any accident occurrences during their space tourism clients are staying to enter these any one of space buildings to visit or play any space entertainment facilities safely, e.g. space vehicle.

So, they must need to ceck anywhere the space planet's places to be ensured safe to build any buildings. Then, they can choose the suitable locations to build space entertainment facilities or buildings more confidently.

In fact, any space entertainment facilities, e.g. space hotels, space farming lands as well as space transportation tools, e.g. spce vehicle, spacecraft , these things will be value to be concerned to any space tourism leisure providers and it is business moral ethic responsibility to every one of them, when they plan to develop their space tourism business in any planets.

(3) Space tourism market competition challenge aspect

Thirdly, any provate space tourism development leisure businesses will face market competitive challenge, such as large spacefaring countries, e.g. US, UK have possible to dominate future space tourism leisure business (government can own space tourism leisure business). They will be main actors in space were nation-states. Large spacefaring counties can build the space vehicles, that can take people and cargo into orbit and to the Moon, or Mars crafted international space law and shaped the main investments in space tourism leisure technology.

So, it is possible that the own space technological developed countries, such as US, UK, these countries governemts will have possible to operate public fund to support space tourism leisure business. It implies that private space tourism leisure businesses will face public space tourism leisure business and themselve private space tourism leisure business market competition in space tourism leisure industry.

If these two countries governments also participate this private space tourism leisure market. It will raise market threats to any private space tourism organizations.

Whether will developed countries governments participate private space tourism market? It is possible that new commercial actors began to enter the space tourism leisure industry, looking to disrupt both space launch services ans use space in new exotic ways. For example, the US government also moved its purposeful degradatoin of the global positioning system (GPS), so US government will have effort to dominate GPS global positioning system communication business also. As this GPS communication business case, future US government has possible to decide to participate space tourism leisure business also.

However, in the future, space tourism leisure industry may contribute even more the developed countries, e.g. American, England economy. Space tourism and resource recovery, e.g. mining on planet, Moons and asteroids in particular may become large parts of that space tourism industry if these countries governments participated to this space tourism industry development. Of course, their viability rests on a range of factors, including costs , future regulation, international market competivitive problems and assumption about space technological development. However, these is increasing optimism in these areas of economic production to bring human space tourism leisure enjoyment and space mining resource development benefits. But the space economy is not just about what happens in orbits or how that alters life on the ground. The growth of this economy can also contribite to new innovations across all future possible unpredictable or undiscovered technological development, instead of space tourism leisure or space mining resource exploitation development.

Consequently, any space development technological governments will have possible to bring economic benefits from either only private space tourism leisure organizations or governments and private space tourism leisure both organizations cooperate to participate to achieve space tourism misson to contribute to global economic development and create new jobs to be employed in space labor supply market.

3.1 Can space tourism business bring
economy benefits

It is fact that space tourism activities have a positive and beneficial impact on eveyday life and society and this help space travelers to understand that, despite the high space ticket prices of any space tourism leisure choices. However, space tourism will bring scientific knowledge and technological knowhow and jobs to bring humn tangible or untangible both benefits. I shall indicate these benefits as below:

Although, space tourism leisure seems only leisure activities to be consumed to satisfy any space tourism individual travelling need. However, it can assign space scientists to research and attempt discovery these intangible benefits: Such as tele-communications revolution, satellite weather forecasting, mapping mineral exploration, water resource management diaster mitigation, national security or other undiscovered untangible benefits. Because every spacecraft needs to plan to fly to space, and it will reach any space planet stations, e.g. Mars, Moon planet when it visits these any one planet, the space scientists can attempt to find new undiscovered space resource , e.g. mining or finding new undiscovered satellite weather forecasting method when they can reach these planets to attempt to do space scientifical investigtion to research new space resource , or find any space stones attack to our methods to avoid earth disaster occurrence (national security mission), instead of the spacecraft catchs space passengers to visit these planets to enjoy these planets space entertainment facilities in their space trip journeys.

(1) On space resource benefit aspect

Hence, the space tourism intangible benefits include: space exploration and international cooperation is developing sophisticted space technologies by nations. For example, the images of distant stars and glaxies using Hubble telescope, research laboratory such as international space station to conduct experiments in biology, human biology, physics, Astronomy and meteorology under microgravity environment and testing of the spacecraft systems will be required for space tourism missions to the Moon and Mars. In the future, human would be able to have unlimited and clean solar energy from space for our industries as well as heating and lighting our homes. In the near future , it would be possible to disposed-off our nuclear waste safely and unexpensively and released towards the sun using a space elevator. We many become a space tourist in earth orbit or on the Moon or Mars. We may carry and extra-terrestial mining and even introduce the development of a multi-planet economy.

(2) On education benefit aspect

Another on education benefit aspect, space tourism can let space travelers to feel actual space learning experiences, during the spacecraft is flying in the space. Their space environment learning experience can include, for example: How many spacecraft have been launched by a given country? How many phone calls are made over a satellite? How many lives could be saved by resue satellites? How they feel differences when they are living in one space hotels, they are swimming in the swimming pools, they are visiting the space garden, they are running in one space sport centers, they are visiting in one space farming land, they are sitting or driving one space vehicle on planet land, or they are catching one spacecraft. These space learning experience will let they feel what the actual differences between space environment and earth environment. It is one humankind learning experience education service in any space planet's Moon or Mars remote areas, bringing information and tourism entertainment facilities to the masses. The space experience learning knowledge can provide data to let these space travelers to know, such as how ships can be safe at sea, monitoring the threat of pollution, how enhancing durable medical instruments for better health-care enabling hikers and skiers to be located when lost, many more. So, it seems space tourism can bring much positive benefits as no negative impact on space activitied has been found by the society , the investments are made by the nations on space activites are justified and not the waste of money.

● What are the tangible social and economic benefits brought from space tourism?

In most advanced economies space tourism or space resource exploitation industry is seen as an enabler that improves lives and helps to develop both economic and social spheres. Space industry economic can include these aspect: Application of space technology to space tourism navigation, meteorological forcasting and broadcast of on live television and internet connectivity to lesser-known applications, such as precision agriculture, transport, tracking, resource extraction and monitoring of utility networks.

Additional application exists in the disaster monitoring and relif, insurance and military applications. Thus, data coming from satellites is important to all economic sectors, making the world a better and safer place.

International space tourism experience would suggest that space travelling leisure businesses deliver value by providing a central point for academia industry , defence and foreign entities to collaborate among themselves and with government and to facilitate the flow of knowledge and capital.

How can space tourism industry maximize the socio-economic benefits? In fact, our growing use of space derived data and systems is our growing dependence on a better and safer sapce planet, e.g. Moon or Mars and to provide space tourism safe services that space travelling service that space traveler all benefit from industry in telecommunication , health, transport , banking , security and climate change monitoring.

The space tourism positive influence result is long term, the positive contribution to our quality of life is real. In other word, the world for space tourism leisure activities is changing the internationally space tourism sector is experiencing a profound revolution.

In conclusion, space tourism leisure countries with historical leadership in space tourism have been under positive as a result of a tough financial environment leading to the definition of their space travelling technology priorities. In the meantime, new space entertainment travelling leaders, such as US, UK , even China, India have ambitions in space tourism through massive investments in the development of their capabilities in space travelling leisure business aspect.

So, the future space travelling entertainment market is large, due to China and India both have many rich people and high income people, who expect to consume in space tourism leisure trip at least one time in their lifes. Consequently, worldwide space tourism entertainment industry players are rethinking their busines models and strategies as they experience discuptive innovations, competitive space tourism entertainment and new drivers impacting the spacecraft and any space entertainment facilities manufacturing on Moon or Mars planet, launch and space tourism entertainment related businesses. Thus, we can in fact in talk about a new space tourism business, in which more and more innovative applications of space tourism data are developed dependence on space tourism data in everyday life rises and increasing share of economic growth relies on the space tourism market both in terms of opportunity benefits , e.g. India and China spce tourism potential market development and any concern space tourism job creation to every countries. Hence, space tourism development can bring positive economic benefits to any countries.

Reference

Cater Iain , Carl 2010, " Steps to space: Opportunities for astro tourism development, tourism management 31 (2010); pp. 838-845; Elsevier Ltd, DOI: 10:1016/j.tourman. 2009.09.001

Collins Patric, Iwasaki Yoichi, Kanayama Hideki, Ohnuki Misuzo 1994, comercial implications of market research on space tourism. journal space technology and sciences , vol. 10 no 2, 94 Autumn, pp.3-11. copyright: Japanese rocket society; available at: www.spacefuture.com/archive/ commercial-implications-of market-research-on-space- tourism.shtml.

Collins Patric, Marita M; Stockmans R. and Kobayahi S. 1996. "Demand for space tourism in America and Japan and its implications for future space activities ". sixth international space conference of Pacific basic societies; Marina del rey; California: Advantages in the Astronautica science (AAS paper no AAS 95-605) vol. 91. pp. 601-610. Available at: http://m.internationalaerospaceconsulting.org/upload/space % 20Future% 20-%20Demand%   20for%20space%   20Tourism%20in% 20America%20Japan.pdf

ESA 2008, " Richard Garriott, millionaire American space tourist. blasks off of international space station". published in 12.11.2008. Huffington post, seen on i01.04.2015; available at: http://www.huffington.com/2008/10/12/richard-garriott-milliona-n-1333940.html.

Klemm, G., & Markkanen, S. (2011). IN A Papathanassis (ed.) The long Tai , tourism (pp.95-103). Weisbaden, Germany : Gabler Verlag; Springer Fachmedien Weiesbaden GmbH.

KSCVC Visitors, 2013; MRI 2013 Market by Market

Von Der Dunk , F. (2012). The integrated approach. Regulating private human spaceflight as space activity, aircraft operation, and high-risk adventure tourism. Acta Astronautica, 92(2), 199-208.

Future space tourism psychology
prediction stragegy

● Psychology and economic environment changing both factors influence whole space tourism market leisure desire

How can psychology method predict space tourism leisure desire? I believe that it has relationship between the space tourism planner and the economic environment as well as his/her psychology as below:

Firstly, on the economic environment influence hand, it includs these both economic situations, either in the good economic environment, many people can earn high income and employers can supply many job number to provide to many people to work, then it will influence the space travelling planner has more space travelling desire. Otherwise, or in the bad economic, less people can earn high income and employers can not supply many job number to provide to many people to work, it will influence the space travelling planner has less space travelling desire.

Secondly, on these both the space travelling planner individual psychology influence hand, the space travelling planner will have these both aspects of individual psychological influence, it includes these both either positive or negative psychological influence aspectsas below:

On the positive psychological influence aspect, if the space travelling planner has confidence to the space travelling leisure company can provide safe, comfortable, good quality of one space travelling trip arrangement, good taste food arrangement, reasonable space ticket price and every reasonable space trip for space hotel living arrangement and space garden and space farming land visiting journey arrangement, even, space swimming pool and space sport centre and space cinema leisure arrangement to let whom to stay on the planet at least one day trip, it means not one short time space trip, e.g. the spacecraft only flies about half hour or one half. It can not fly to the planet to arrive its space station destination to stay to let the space travelling planner to live at the space hotel at least one night. Then the space travelling planner will have more desire to choose to catch the space tourism leisure company's spacecraft to travel to space.

Otherwise, on the negative psychological influence aspect, if the space travelling planner lacks confidence to the space travelling leisure company can provide safe, comfortable, good quality of one space travelling trip arrangement, good taste food arrangement, reasonable space ticket price and every reasonable space trip for space hotel living arrangement and space garden and space farming land visiting journey arrangement, even, space swimming pool and space sport centre and space cinema leisure arrangement to let whom to stay on the planet at least one day trip, it means not one short time space trip, e.g. the spacecraft only flies about half hour or one half. It can not fly to the planet to arrive its space station destination to stay to let the space travelling planner to live at the space hotel at least one night. Then the space travelling planner will have less desire to choose to catch the space tourism leisure company's spacecraft to travel to space.

Hence, it seems economic environment changing factor and the space travelling planner's confidence factor to the space tourism leisure providers will influence the whole space travelling market whose space travelling consumer's space travelling leisure consumption desire to be more or less. So, any one space tourism provider can not neglect these both factors how to influence whose customer consumption desire.

● space tourism strategy

Future any space tourism leisure business needs have good business plan to outline the space tourism leisure business in these aspects , such as: different space tourism destinations of every space tourism journey, technical , financial and regulatory factors for growing space tourism leisure consumption into any one kind of unique artificial intelligent space tourism journey for identified passenger target group.

All how to design one space tourism business development plan to attempt to predict whether what trends will influence how every different kinds of identified space tourism journey in order to achieve passenger number growing aim as well as how to achieve one attractive space tourism leisure to satisfy future space tourism passenger individual space travel needs more easily.

I shall indicate what aspects to future every space tourism traveler who will consider in order to reduce the space tourism traveler personal worry to catch any pace boats to leave our Earth to fly to other planets to travel.

I recommend that any space tourism leisure organizations need to concern these aspects in their space tourism leisure business plan as below:

(1) safe space tourism journey

On first aspect concerns safe space tourism journey plan to let all space tourism travelers will considerate safe issue. They must ensure space boats that is safe to catch them to fly to planets in their space journeys. So, any space tourism leisure business will utilize previous flight rated and proven technologies to form the basis for manufacturing spacecraft vehicles, and will incorporate the latest modern avionics and flight systems for ensuring safety, reliability and economical operation in order to reduce any space tourism traveler personal worry to catch any spacecraft.

So, the space tourism safe journey plan is one very important factor to influence space tourism consumer number for them if any one of space tourism leisure business hoped they can grow the space tourism consumer number for long term. For example, the space boat flight hardware must often be maintained at the space station. It is needed to be considered by space boat experts as risky, extremely expensive and potentially sensitive. To aims to ensure spacecraft will offer an economical and safe alternative for any satellite manufacturers and other space tourism entertainment organizations have a desire or requirement for space tourism flight.

(2) reduction cost expense plan

On second aspect concerns reduction cost expense plan, any space tourism entertainment organizations need have the experience and capacity for safely launching a fully loaded , including space tourism passengers and passenger individual cargo for every spacecraft tourism journey. As a result of outsourcing the launch role to a major contractor, the space tourism pilot can concentrate on space boat crews flight training, planning space tourism passenger cargo capacity and preparing space flight manifests , and will as a result, avoid the expense of maintaining a launch operation on a daily basis. In addition, by outsourcing the spacecraft manufacturing, it can avoid spending millions of dollar on facilities and equipment infrastructure and engineering manufacturing expertise.

(3) achieve any space tourism mission plan

On third aspect concerns how to achieve any space tourism mission. Every space tourism mission must be ensure that reliable service is provided to satisfy every space tourism passenger personal space traveler needs and let them to enjoy in their whole space tourism journey, let them to catch a big aircraft in comfortable environment of technologically sophisticated space boat, reasonable and competitive every time space tourism flight ticket price plan is developed and properly revised every time space tourism ticket price when performing their assigned every different space tourism journey mission.

Hence, the space tourism leisure company will provide one careful selected space tourism destination , e.g. Mar planet space tourism journey, Moon planet space tourism journey or no any space destination journey, it means that the space craft only needs to fly one circle around between Earth and Moon space journey etc. that are capable of meeting the requirements of travelling into Earth orbit. So, any space tourism journey must emphasize affordability, reliability, safety, customer service and responsiveness in responding to every client's space tourism journey requirements. Hence, any one of space tourism journey must have clear space journey mission and objective to satisfy any space traveler client target needs.

Methods to raise space
traveler number

Future space tourism will be one kind of new travel leisure market for any new space travel leisure companies to enter this undiscovered market in the beginning. However, how to predict future 10 to 20 years , even more space traveler number that is one important issue to any new space tourism leisure companies.

I think that space tourism leisure companies need to define what kinds of space travel leisure service to be provided to space travelling passengers, however, what age group of space passengers who will be their space travelling target client. For example, their space travel leisure must provide any flight operation that takes one or more passengers beyond the altitude of 100 km and thus into space to let space travelling passengers who have fun, exciting space travelling feeling.

Anyway, for any kind of space tourism (leisure space travel) journey, space tourism leisure company needs anyone to be bring customer satisfaction, it is a plan or predictive methods to measure how to let every space travelling passenger to feel comfortable when they are catching the spacecraft (space flying product) and they can have enjoyable and fun or exciting feeling when they have need providing any space tourism journey, services meet or surpass customer expectations.

Thus, any space tourism leisure company needs to evaluate the degree of every time space tourism journey's customer satisfaction and customer satisfaction is also always evaluated in relationship to the every time ticket price of the space tourism journey. So, the space tourism leisure company will predict the next time of what the space tourism journey of passenger number is more accurate, after it has evaluated what degree of every time space tourism journey's customer satisfaction is. It aims to gather their opinions to find which aspects that they need to revise, e.g. choosing where will be the next time space tourism journey destination, how to improve spacecraft staff's service attitude and performance to serve to their space tourism passengers when they are catching the spacecraft, to evaluate whether the spacecraft can provide comfortable and safe environment to let them to catch in order to let the next time space travelling passengers can feel satisfactory and enjoyable when they are catching the space tourism leisure's spacecraft to fly to anywhere in space.

In general, the expectation of factors space passengers include the following customer value elements, such as below:

- viewing space and the Earth.
- experiencing weightlessness and being able to float freely in zero gravity.
- experiencing pre-flight astronaut training and related sensations.
- communicating from space to significant others.
- being able to discuss the adventure in an informed way.
- having astronaut like documentation and memorabilia.

These objectives need to be combined with, sometimes conflicting constraints, such as guaranteed safe return, limited training time, reasonable comfort, and minimum medical restrictions. All these above issues which will be every space travelling passenger considerate matters before they choose the space tourism leisure company to catch its spacecraft to fly to space. So, all these factors will influence the next time space passenger number. Any space tourism leisure company can not neglect how to solve these all matters before they decide when their next time space tourism journey to be achieved.

Consequently, if the space craft tourism leisure company could revise what aspects of its last space tourism journey to find what are its wrong or weakness or unattractive challenges to cause any one space travelling passenger who feels unsatisfactory. Then, it can have more effort to concentrate on improving its next space tourism journey to raise its space tourism service performance level , e.g. people, food, leisure etc. service aspects and its space tourism product quality level, e.g. proving comfortable spacecraft facilities to let space travelling passengers to catch in whole spacecraft tourism journey. Then, it will have more confidence to achieve the raising space travelling passenger number.

● What is the prediction space travelling passenger desire method ?
The prediction space travelling passenger individual desire method can be one survey investigation method. When every time spacecraft finishes space tourism journey mission, after all space tourism passengers catch the spacecraft to arrive earth from space. When they arrive earth space station destination, then the space tourism leisure company can arrange survey investigation staffs to enquire their feeling for this time space tourism journey immediately.
The survey content can include as below:
Do you feel satisfactory or unsatisfactory to which aspects of this time space tourism journey?
(1) On service aspect questions include as below:
(a) Do you feel space food taste is good?
(b) Do you enjoy this time space tourism journey arrangement?
(c) Do you feel satisfactory to space staff
service performance?
(d) If you have unsatisfactory feeling for any one of above questions, which aspect issue cause you feel unsatisfactory to explain to let us to know in order to us to revise our service performance.

(2) On product aspect questions include as below:
(a) Do you feel comfortable when you are catching our spacecraft in whole space tourism journey?
(b) If you feel comfortable , may you explain the reasons what aspects of our spacecraft has weakness to cause you feel uncomfortable?
(c) Do you feel safe when you are catching our spacecraft in whole space tourism journey?
(d) If you feel unsafe, may you explain the reasons what aspects of our

spacecraft has weakness to cause you feel unsafe?

Finally, we thank your ideas to be given to let us know how to improve our every time future space tourism journey in order to find what challenge cause our service performance and product quality which can not satisfy your needs. So, we shall improve to avoid future challenges continue occur. Our mission is achievement of 100% satisfactory level to our every space travelling passenger individual feeling. Also, we hope that you can choose our space tourism leisure service again, when you have another time space tourism leisure desire need. However, we shall revise to improve our service performance and product quality to be better, after collecting your ideas from this time survey investigation. I think you spend time to give your ideas from this survey investigation faithfully.

So, survey investigation method will be one important idea gathering tool to help any space tourism leisure company to revise the weaknesses to raise or improve future every time space tourism journey service performance and product quality to achieve raising competitive effort in this new space tourism leisure market.

Hence, survey investigation method will be the best idea gathering method to predict how space travelling passenger emotion or desire need will change in order to achieve the objective of raising every time space tourism journey future space travelling passenger number more easily for every space tourism leisure company.

CHAPTER FOUR

Technology how helps old leisure businesses innovation

● The prediction of price factor influences space traveler number

The space tourism leisure organizations indicate the total cost of a trip into space is rapidly coming down from the initial price level of about US$600,000, it is obvious that the space travelling customer base is going to be rather small. Typical customers tend to belong to the top 1% income bracket. They also indicate that the price comes down , it is expected that new space travelling customer groups will enter the space tourism leisure market.

Typical new customers include people in other brackets with one-of-a kind incomes, such as inheritance or business sold. There are indications that those types of customers are becoming interested in spending on an once-in-a lifetime space experience. Therefore, the growth of the space tourism market is highly sensitive to customer satisfaction and how it is communicated through various media.

This will establish the status factors of space tourism and corresponding brand reputation service providers. They also suggest that any operator monitors space travelling customer satisfaction closely, as it will help developing increasingly accurate estimates of how the space tourism leisure market will develop.

Hence, it seems that every time space tourism journey price variable factor will influence the time space tourism of customer individual leisure desire and the space tourism passenger number. For example, the minimum price goal foe a variable space tourism business is currently estimate to be below US$3000-4000/kg for a round -trip depending on variable configuration and operation size. At this price, they estimate that somewhat over 1 % of the high income earners are potential customers.

However, for significant volume growth the longer term goal should be below US$2000/kg for a typical passenger, baggage and supplies. The lower price will probably open space tourism to a broader population, expanding the customer base and altering expectations. beyond this point space tourism will become into a travelling competitive leisure commodity, price competition will ensure and service providers need to rethink their space tourism marketing and branding and price strategies.

I shall also recommend how to attract the potential customers successfully. First, space operators need to pay special attention to the right level of customer services. Second, various preparatory customer operations cost, such as a travel to the launch site, space tourism destination accommodation, pre-flight training, medical check-ups and equipment my add up to between 10 to 15 % of the actual space travel cost. Thurs, solving the right balance between services offered and cost of client operation in order to earn the largest intangible benefits, such as loyalty, confidence, leisure enjoyment, comfortable space travelling journey as well as tangible benefits, such as profit, spacecraft manufacturing facilities, space stations, space hotels , space swimming pools, space gardens, space cinema etc. which are built to similar to earth building facilities to satisfy space travelers' needs.

The influential factors persuade travelers choose space tourism

Nowadays, our earth is no longer an adventurous enough place for some experienced tourists. Space tourism will be a new sector of adventure tourism, which is in the near future will be fast becoming a new tourism leisure opportunity for experiencing the unknown. Of one day, space tourism is able to reach the mass tourism phase, due to improved safety and decreased operation costs, a future space tourist will possibly only need minimal training to cope with the zero cost.

Space tourism is quite well established with visits to space attraction and launch sites, and it is a wealthy trips to the international space station for any space tourism travelers. However, if any space tourism leisure companies can attempt to find what the most influential factors are to persuade travelers feel attraction more than travelling in our earth.

It aims to let travelers to choose space travelling more than earth travelling when they feel travelling leisure need. I shall indicate what will be the most important influential factors to persuade travelers to choose space tourism more than earth tourism as below:

Firstly, I shall argue that the majority of different new space tourism journey destinations will be needed to find to satisfy different aged space travelers and different income space tourism consumers' needs. For example, the rich people have effort to consume longer time and reach any space tourism destinations where are far away from our earth of their every space tourism journey.

Otherwise, the middle income people will choose shorter space tourism journey distance from our earth and short time space tourism journey. Also, younger space tourism clients can accept more longer journey time, exciting fast speed spacecraft flying journey. Otherwise, old space tourism clients can only accept comfortable and shorter time safe space journey. So, it seems that safety, comfortable feeling, shorter time space tourism journey won't be one important influential factor to excite any young people who choose to consume space tourism leisure. Otherwise, safety, comfortable feeling, shorter time space tourism journey will be one important influential factor to excite any old people who choose to consume space tourism leisure.

Secondly, the another most important influential factor to excite space travelers to choose space tourism , it concerns whether the space travelers will feel what tourists benefits can be earned from a substantial variety of destinations choice. In general, space tourism with those of aviation, space travelers will hope space tourism will be travelling distances by air in a very short time, safely and comfortably, to bring them to arrive any space planet destinations when spacecraft reaches any space stations to stay in any space destinations.

Hence, space destination factor will bring important influential choice to any space destination journeys. As a result of the space technological tourism boom, the number of potential different space destination, choice attractions have grown with far fewer places on earth to which human do have access yet. However, the ultimate different space destinations to which many of us dream is not on earth, but as least 100 km above us, anywhere in space any planets.

If the space tourism leisure company can provide different space tourism destination choices to young or old age both space traveler target consumer groups. They will feel a real holiday when they will be able to enjoy a great image of the earth from planets. It might mean that every space tourism journey can provide different space tourism destination to let space travelers have another new travelling destinations where are far from our earth anywhere.

Hence, the different space tourism destinations will give them an unforgettable adventure. Think of how it would be to be able to check in at a " billion strategy" luxury hotel in space one planet, it means that the space planet destination can provide one luxury hotel to let space travelers to live one night or more in the space planet destination, how it would be to schedule the space traveler' vacation at one of the space tourism leisure company luxury resorts on the Moon or Mars.

This images seem from science fiction movies, but one should not forget that 100 years ago, the Wright brothers, aviation pioneers inventors and builders of the air plane, would not have imagined how, every day it is possible that future spacecraft can fly to any planets to let human have chance to stay in the space hotel one night or more.

Consequently, space destination choice and space tourism journey service performance, aviation safety, ticket price and leisure satisfactory feeling which will be important influential factors to attract future space travelers to choose space tourism leisure to replace earth tourism leisure in future one day.

● Raising space tourism leisure
consumption strategies

Although, space tourism industry is a real enjoyment and exciting travelling leisure to human. It is possible that human will choose to consume space tourism leisure to replace earth tourism leisure, if human felt that earth tourism leisure is not attractive to them to consume to go to anywhere to travel in their leisure time.

But, I believe that space tourism industry has still many factors to influence human to choose to consume space tourism leisure, even they will consider space tourism leisure consumption I is only one time space tourism in their life time. Hence, space tourism companies ought achieve this aim to persuade or attract everyone prefer to spend space tourism leisure at least one time in their life, then it can represent success. However, I think to achieve this aim, it has these challenges to influence their success, even they believe space tourism leisure business is one potential attractive travel entertainment business. These challenges include such as: expensive space tourism ticket price issue, catching spacecraft safe issue, space traveler personal body health issue, age issue, family and friend relationship influence issue, working time and holiday time arrangement issue, the space trip arrangement issue, weather issue etc. different challenges, which will have possible to influence every space tourism planner either who decide change to cancel the time space tourism plan, or forgive to choose space tourism leisure in their life forever.

Hence, how to raise space tourism leisure consumption desire will be one considerable matter for any space tourism leisure businessmen. I shall indicate my personal three aspect of strategical opinions to let them to know how to raise every space tourism planner individual space tourism leisure consumption desire to avoid every time space tourism passenger number will have decrease failure chance as below:

● (1) Strategic opinion

On the first aspect of strategic opinion, I feel that the space education tutor can teach new space knowledge to let every space traveler to learn any new space and earth knowledge during he/she is catching on the spacecraft in personal contact learning experience environment which can raise space tourism consumption desire. The reason is because the space tourism leisure traveler can raise extra space and earth learning knowledge when they can catch the spacecraft to fly and contact the space environment to learn and feel what the differences are between space and earth by himself or herself. Hence, it is very attractive to the space traveler student target group and I believe that their parents will encourage their sons or daughters to participate the time of space trip and they are more preferable to help them to buy the time space trip ticket, due to their sons and daughters can learn any space knowledge when they are studying. Moreover, every space traveler will feel surprise to learn any new space and earth knowledge from the space tutor's teaching, due to he/she is unknown that this space travel trip includes learning space and earth knowledge.

I suggest that the space tourism leisure businessmen can give learning opportunity to every travel trip space travelers to feel that this space actual environment can bring what disadvantages or advantages to influence our earth when they are catching aircraft to fly to space to travel in every space trip. The space and earth learning knowledge can include these two aspects of space learning knowledge and experience below:

On the teaching of space environment learning knowledge hand, the topics can include as below:

Firstly the space learning topic can concern how space environment influences water and hydrated minerals change , they can learn what our drinking water function how is applied to space environment. For example, in the space environment, they can learn and attempt to feel that how water can be used in protecting astronauts against harmful radiation from the sun and cosmic rays by cloaking spacecraft with a thin layer of water in the actual space environment as well as the space travelers can also feel water is same as fuel when they are catching the spacecraft, they can feel the water is heavy to transport into space when they are catching the spacecraft to fly to space during their whole space tourism journey.

Moreover, when their spacecraft reaches anyone of planets and it stays on the planet's space station, e.g. Moon space station. They can learn how to attempt to contact the hydrated minerals to learn and feel what they contained in some asteroids may be possible sources of water and fuel in the actual space environment. When they are walking in actual space environment, such as Moon planet, they can contact or touch this hydrated minerals to learn how water molecules can be extracted and separated chemically to produce hydrogen fuel knowledge in the actual space environment. This is one exciting space learning experience to the space travelling student passengers.

Secondly the space learning topic can concern how human fights space threats , even when their whole space leisure journey, the space science teacher can let the space trip student passengers to feel that they are learning new space knowledge between the space science teacher and whose space trip student passengers. Such as how to protect our earth knowledge: Teaching them to know when will be threats to our earth from space. The space science teacher can explain how this space threating environment influences our life safety and let them to feel that a mass extinction can be triggered if an asteroid 10 kilometers across hit the earth. Even being the apex species in the food chain did not space carnivorous dinosaurs from such disaster, who knows if this terrifying scene won't happen before our eyes? So, the space travelers can image and feel how the space threating environment can influence their life safety in the actual space environment as well as the space science teacher can let whose space travelers to feel and image the actual earth disaster will possible happen suddenly to let they feel afraid in the actual space environment. Also the space science teacher can teach how our earth can fright the space stones attack to let the space traveler to know, when an impactor targets an asteroid for a controlled well-times wallop. The collision will change the asteroid's momentum, deflecting it from its original orbital path which intersects with that of the earth. So, at the moment, the space travelers can image they are a larger spacecraft near an asteroid which can also change the path. Given enough time, the gravitational pull from the spacecraft will be able to steer the asteroid away from the earth. So, every space traveler will feel that they are catching the spacecraft in the safe space environment to avoid the Earth disaster from space sudden unpredictable attack.

It is more fun real space tourism knowledge learning feel to let every space traveler has chance to learn any new space science knowledge when he/she is catching the spacecraft to fly to space to travel. Hence, one successful space trip ought include trip and learning experience both contents in order to raise every the space tourism planner individual space trip consumption desire.

● (2) Strategic opinion

On the second aspect of strategic opinion, space tourism leisure companies need to let planning travelers feel that anyone of space tourism leisure is very different to general tourism leisure. In general, tourism leisure is visiting at least one night for leisure and holiday, business or other tourism purposes in Earth only. Otherwise, space tourism leisure is other kind of an unique trip leisure or entertainment method, e.g. the space traveler can catch the spacecraft to visit any planets to stay to live at the planet's space hotel at least one night, e.g. Future potential populated Moon or Mars space hotel space trip. Moreover, the space travel companies ought give chance to let them to feel what weightless feeling is in weightlessness environment when they are walking on Moon or other planets in possible. Even, they can attempt to build these entertainment facilities, instead of space hotels, such as space swimming pools, space gardens, space cinema etc. building facilities. It aims to let them to feel what the differences between Earth and space life when they are walking on the Moon, when they are swimming on the space pools, when they are living in space hotels, when they are watching movies in space cinemas, when they are seeing flowers and different species of planets and fruits. e.g. oranges, apples, bananas, and vegetable and potatoes and tomatoes in space gardens. It is very exciting and fun space trip life experience between one days to seven days. So, they believe that they must not feel these space life experience if they do not choose to participate this time space trip planning journey by the space trip company preparation.

Also, due to that the space tourism passengers need to the pre-flight checks and training before they ensure to qualify to permit to participate the space trip. So space travel companies need to concern how to take care their health check and training matter considerately. It aims to let every space traveler will feel a market segment with fitness and extreme experiences as well as he/she will become popular with a market segment passenger to the space tourism leisure company, although he/she must not guarantee to pass the space training and/or pre-flight health checks to permit to participate the space trip. However, he/she can believe that he/she is one worth space travelling passenger to the space tourism leisure company, even this time pre-flight health check or/and the short time space trip training requirements are failure. However, the space tourism leisure company must need to let all pre-flight health check and space trip training passengers to feel that it is only one space tourism which can give them and let customers view the space travel is as the ultimate showcase for health, even though a majority of the population can pass the pre-flight medical and other tests in order to raise their confidence and safety to catch the spacecraft to fly to space to travel when they are confirmed to pass these tests to permit to catch the spacecraft later.

In general, the expectations of future space passengers include the following customer value elements, such as below:

- Viewing space and the Earth.
- Experiencing weightlessness and experiencing pre-flight astronaut training and related sensations.
- Communicating from space to significant others.
- Being able to discuss the adventure in an informed way.
- Having astronaut-like documentation and memorabilia.
- Enjoying one exciting and fun space trip.

However, instead of considering these objectives need to be combined with, sometimes conflicting , constraints such as guaranteed safe, return , limited training time, reasonable comfort, and minimum medical restrictions. So, space tourism companies need to reduce every space traveler individual worries before they decide to make the time of space tourism journey. Then, it can increase their confidence to raise their space tourism consumption desire more successfully.

Consequently, instead of these consideration, a space travel operator must pay attention to the total customer experience over the entire customer process, starting from how the service is presented, proposed and sold. The service package must include training, instructions, travel to the launch site and various post. Travel activities to generate maximum customer satisfaction and brand building opportunity.

(3) Strategic opinion

On the final aspect of strategic opinion, I think any space tourism companies space tourism companies need to consider every time space tourism ticket price and space tourism trip issues. It is important factor to influence every space traveler individual consumption desire. Due to space trip ticket price must be more expensive to compare common Earth trip travelling ticket price, so this kind of tourism leisure market target customer will be the rich and high income customer group.

On the space trip ticket challenge issue, despite that fact the total cost of a trip into space is rapidly coming down from the initial price level of about US$60,000, it is obvious that the customer base is going to be rather small and the client target customer is only high income or rich consumer group. Typical customers tend to belong to the top of the top 1% income bracket. So, ensures that space traveler number must be less than common Earth traveler number.

Also, such as the space trip ticket price, it is expected that new middle rich level or middle high level income customer target group will enter the space trip leisure market, when every space trip ticket price falls down about 1% Typical new customers include people in other income brackets with one-of-a-kind incomes, such as inheritance or business sold space traveler target group. These people will be space travel new client group, when its every space trip ticket price can be reduced to close 1 to 2 % nearly. If any space tourism leisure companies expect to attract new rich and/or high income target customer group to choose any one kind of space trip journey planning to consume.

These are indications that these types of customers are becoming interested in spending on an once-in-a-lifetime space experience. Therefore, the growth of the space tourism market is highly sensitive to customer satisfaction and how it is communicated through the various media. This will establish the status –factor of space tourism, and corresponding brand reputation of service providers. The minimum price goal for a variable space tourism business is currently estimate to be below US$3-4000/kg for a round-trip depending on vehicle configuration. So, space travel leisure companies need to concern every round space trip cost, it can depend on the space vehicle number and weight issue to influence every space trip ticket price variable to achieve how much it can earn.

On space journey design factor aspect, it includes these different facilities aspects how to design, because future space travelling consumers will concern whether the space travel company can provide special entertainment to satisfy their needs. The facilities include as below:

How to design space hotels to let them to live in comfortable space environment and eat the best taste and fresh food quality when the cookers need to cook in the space hotel in the space environment? How to design space swimming pools to let them to swim in safe space environment? How to design space sport centers to let them to run more easily in one space sport warm and safe environment? How to design one space garden to let them to see different species of Earth flowers, or plants? How to design one space farming land to let them to see different species of Earth fruits, vegetables, tomatoes, potatoes etc. fresh foods growth in warm and safe space farming land environment? How to design one space cinema to let them to watch movies in one safe and warm space cinema environment? All these facilities will be any one of future space trip's' important and attractive space trip leisure facilities to influence every space traveler to choose to buy the space tourism leisure company's space trip leisure service.

Instead of these space building entertainment facilities, they also need to concern how the space vehicle entertainment tools are provided the entertainment service to satisfy their needs. When the space travelers can sit on the space vehicles to move on any planets' lands, such as Moon. A number of space vehicle options exist in the market, mainly differing based on the seat capacity as well as the in-flight experience level offered. The typical space vehicle solution is a small, relatively light weight spacecraft taking between 2 to 10 passengers. The number of passengers depends on the service level, amenities and extra offered. The trip typically lasts about 10 hours and of which about 4 hours are spent in space. The main attraction is the weightless time after in space. The main attraction is the weightless time after re-entry has started. It is a rather low-G technology and therefore the medical requirements for participants are nor very high.

Consequently, the space vehicles, space leisure building facilities, the space trip reasonable price ticket level, every safe space trip journey arrangement, clean and fresh and good taste space food arrangement, space traveler individual real learning experience etc. these factors will be the main influential factors to raise the space tourism leisure company's competitive effort and the space traveler consumer individual consumption desire to the space tourism leisure company in the future.

Space travel markting strategy

Any space travel organization needs have good marketing strategy to prepare how to operate its space travelling leisure business in order to attract many space travelling clients to choose its space travelling service. I shall indicate these different strategies aspects whey they are needed to be concerned as below:

(1) On concept of spacecraft design aspect

Firstly, on concept aspect, any one space travelling leisure company needs have at least one spacecraft to catch clients to fly to space to travel. So how to design the spacecraft and its quality and safety and comfortable environment spacecraft machine concept aspect issue which is one challenge to be concerned. Because many space travelling passengers ususally concern whether the spacecraft is safe, comfortable , good quality, as well as the space travelling leisure providers also need to concern whether the spacecraft is less time and energy saving efficient use, less manufactory operating cost and durable.

In general, space travelling leisure provider expects the spacecraft or spacecraft vehicle can be uesed long time. The spacecraft will be expected to utilize previous flight rated and proven technologies to from the basis for manufacturing spacecraft vehicles , and will incorporate the latest modern avionics and flight system for answering safety, reliability and economical operation.

In general, the spacecraft will be designed to carry two crew and approximately, 10,000 pounds of cargo, depending on the ultimate weight of the spacecraft. Relying on flight hardware to maintain the space station, such as Moon or Mar space station is fpr any space travelling spacecrafts to reach these space travelling destinations to stay, it is also need to consider by many space travelling experts as risky, extremely, expensive cost sensitive for any space station travelling destination design arrangement in order to future every spacecraft can fly to any planets to stay on its space station safely.

● Outsourcing spacecraft concept design strategy

As a result, outsourcing strategy is one good method to help them to reduce cost in order to achieve to let every space travel passenger has safe space journey experience and capacity for safely launching a fully loaded (including crew and cargo). Outsourcing strategy is the launch role to a major contracor, they can concentrate on crew flight training, planning all passnegers and cargo capacoty, and preparing flight manifests, and will as a result, avoid the expense of maintaining a launch operation on a daily basis. In addition, by outsoucing the spacecraft manufacturing, the space travelling provider can avoid spending millions of dollars on facilities and equipment infrastructure and engineering manufacturing expertise.

(2) On deciding misson aspect

Secondly, on mission aspect, any space travelling journey needs have a clear mission to be planned how to achieve in order to ensure every space travelling passenger feel satisfactory in the space travelling journey. So, every whole space travelling journey arrangement, e.g. where will be the space travelling destination, how to check every space travelling planned passengers' bodies whether who are health to catch spacecraft to fly to space to travel or how to train every space travelling planned passenger to ensure whom can permit to catch spacecraft to fly to space to travel, how to arrange every space travelling journey entertainment and facilities to let either young or old age target passenger to enjoy the space trip to feel satisfactory, how to arrange different days of every space trip.

In the last few years, Virgin Galactic has been making new's headlines with its promises to provide space travel services, and announcement that it will soom offer, at quite a hefty price, trips to sub-orbit. It is generally agreed that sub-orbit exists 100 kilometres above the earth's sea-level (Von Der Dunk, 2012). Hence, Virgin Galactic will provide travel to where customers may experience weightlessness, as well as the sight of earth's curvature. Even more interesting is that Virgin Galactic is not the only company with such a mission,there are a few more that wish to offer the same type of service. For example, some companies even aim to provide an orbital type of flight.

Orbit flight suggests that humans would venture into outer space, where they might either orbit the earth or board the international space station (hereinafter: ISS). In addition, some envision space hotels, moon visitations and mining asteroids. Although at first such statement might seem for one must point out that a "space hotel" is already in earth's orbit and that diligent progress through flight tests is almost made the commercial aspect of regular space travel a reality; it is only the question of time and readiness for the companies to make their long-awaited and open a new industry of present day economics (Klemm & Markkanen, 2011; Berry , 2012).

So, every space travelling mission is to ensure that reliable, technologically-sophisicated competitively-priced flight certified spacecraft are designed and properly maintained when performing their every assigned space travelling journey mission. The space traveller leisure provider will need to provide a carefully selected array of techologies that are capable of meeting the requirements of travelling into earth orbit. It will emphasize affordability, reliability, safety, customer service and responsiveness in responding to customer's space travelling requirements.

For this space tourism leisure mission example, it many include these objectives , such as below:

One trip into space, sending a space vehicle of a certain make and with a specify capacity on a space mission, provides the various grades of a core service, such as a space mission including issues such as waiting and delivery times, personal attention and advice, amenities and facilities, ensure quality assurance, it is the planned and system activities implemented in a quality system. So that quality requirements for a product or service will be fulfilled. It aims at preventing high-risk adverse events, or reducing thei impact, provides excellent customer satisfaction, it is a measure of how products and services meet the space travelling customer expectations, customer satisfaction is also always evaluated in relationship of every space travelling ticket price of the space travelling entertainment service and spacecraft product comfortable environment feeling and good leisure arrangement for every space travelling leisure journey.

(3) On space tourism leisure organization managment aspect

Thirdly, on space tourism leisure organization management aspect, it is also important to influence efficient and excellent space service performance to be provided to satisfy every space travel organization management team needs to be consists of experienced professionals who have successfully management and operated companies specializing in the aerospace industry for a number of years.

Their knowledge and contacts within the space industry will prove invaluable in assisting the space tourism leisure provider in the achievement of its goals and objectives. In individuals on the team components that up a spacecraft tourism development organization, and have unique experience in the design, construction, operations and maintenance of the major functions will developing spacecraft for launching into orbit. Every spacecraft will be built and maintained utilizing the same high standards of quality, within budget and well within time constraints.

Hence, every space tourism provider needs have one excellent management leaders to manage every space tourism service staffs to serve passengers in order to achieve excellent service performance to let them every one to feel satisfactory, during their every space tourism journey (trip).

(4) On target audience prediction aspect

On target audience prediction aspect, every space trip needs have identifies target travelling passenger in order to concentrate to choose the most popular and satisfactory space travelling journey for their identified needs.

For primary audiences example, it can include space enthusiasts and educational families both. Space enthusiasts target are usually young people and they are only 20% over 65 age old people target space ethusiasts who will be the future potential space tourism target consumers as well as the educational families target who will aspect owning educational experience for children , who is the explicit reason to visit space, either he/she has interest in history of space exploration or he/she has interest in future of space exploration or he/she feels that spce trip looked like fun.

KSCVC Visots (2013) indicated that future top markets, ranked by high visitation against space enthusiasts and educational families space tourism passengers, the US cities will include: Orlando, NYC, Miami, Tampa Bay, Chicago, West plam, Philadelphia, Atlanta, Boston, Washington, DC and San Francisco cities. So, future US space travelling market will be the top one in the world.

(5) On space objective aspect

On space objective aspect, instead of any one space tourism leisure organization concerns how to achieve its mission to satisfy all space tourism passengers leisure needs. Although, it is the major missin for space tourism leisure industry. But they can not neglect what the objectives are in order to develop or achieve long term space tourism leisure missions more easily.

The objectives main open space key issues can include such as: Providing an adequate supply of land to meet the future needs of strategic opn space links, natural areas and recreational facilities on any future space tourism destinations, increasing pressure for public access to open space areas with conservation values, competing interests between adjoining land use and development on public open space and its user groups, use of public open space and recreational resources for drainage purposes, raising higher space traveller hotel residential development placing increased pressure on the demand for public open space planet land use aim and developing public open space mor intensive leisure and sport activities on any future new space tourism planet destinations.

When the space tourism leisure providers have long term objectives to attempt to solve above these any one of key issues. It will ahve a more clear objective to achieve its long term space tourism leisure business market. It's long term objectives can include such as below:

To identify existing and future active and passive recreation needs and social trends of future space tourism visitors; to provide a wide range of high quality and accessible public open space public land areas to encourage physical activity and social interaction to meet the existing and future needs of space travelling visitors; to identify existing gaps in the public open space network and develop any different kinds of space trip arrangement to satisfy the different identified target space traveller individual needs; to protect enhance and increase landcrapt values of public open space land use; to recognize the hierarchy of public open space assets; equitably distributing open space resources; access to facilities and a diverse range of opportunities to incorporate the drainage function in public open space travelling destination areas without detriment to safely, environmental, visual and recreational values.

So, these development of any space planets howo to use their lands objectives will bring long term space travelling destination beneficial advantages to raise to build the space hotels, space swimming pools, space gardens, space cinemas, space sport places to let future space travelers can stay in Mars or Moon planet destinations to enjoy these leisure facilities and they can feel which are similar to our earth leisure facilities attractively.

These space buildings are important to attract future space travellers to catch spacecraft to fly to Mars or Moon planet to travel in possible because it is fun and exciting space trip when these leisure facilities can be built on Moon or Mars to let space travellers to stay short days in either these two planets to live their space hotels. So how to build any one of these space leisure building which is another important objective for any future space tourism leisure business, instead of how to arrange any space destination trip objective. So, any space tourism leisure provider ought not neglect how to achieve these two main space tourism objectives.

However, these are key questions continually asked regarding the viability of space tourism. They concern financial, marketing and political communities. Their concerns can be best addredded in a properly, comprehensive business plan. Some questions can not be answered definitively at this time. Hoever, knowledge of the concerns and developing space businesses in any space traveling leisure planning stages and efforts to raise capital in the following questions, every spce tourism leisure business leader needs to concern this questions as below:

Can the space tourism industry into a profitable enonomic industry?

Are challenges related to financing, marketing, business methodologies or a combination of all of these facets?

Can the proponents of space tourism to be proven business tools and methodologies in their presentation of an acceptable business plan?

Can at least a cost effective, certified passenger space tourism journey to be developed for space tourism?

What effects will influence space-tourism businesses of NASA begins selling seats on the US space shuttle to civilian space tourists?

All above questions will be every new space tourism leisure businessman who needs to concern questions in order to achieve whose marketing strategy more successfully. Consequently, marketing strategy is important to be prepared in order to follow corrective steps to achieve every space tourism leisure business missions and objectives more easily.

● Space tourism leisure behavioral economic
consumption model

In space tourism leisure industry, due to every time space trip needs the space travelling planner to plan how much budget to consume expensive spce ticket price. So, it seems that the target customers will be rich or high income level young people or the retirement rich old people target customer group.

So, it brings this question: How to persuade these rich or high income young people or rich retirement old people to prefer to spend spce tourism leisure at least one time in their life?

It is one valuabe research question to every future space tourism leisure provider. I shall indicate the successful factors to analyze how to persuade them to accept this kind of potential space travelling leisure in behavioral economic personal consumption view point, in order to explain the cause and effect relationship between of these factors as below:

(1) Economic environment variable factor

Firstly, it is economic environment variable factor whether it can influence to space tourism leisure consumption changing. As I discuss about economic environment variable issue will influence consumption behavior changing. For space tourism leisure case, it is not now kind of essential consumption leisure product to every one. So , even the rich or high income people who will be influences to seek this kind of leisure to play, it the economic environment is improved, it will influence they have positive attitude and interest to choose this kind of leisure consumption. However, if the economic environment is worse, it will influence they have negative attitude and no interest to choose this kind of leisure consumption, due to space travel is one kind of expensive leisure consumption to every one.

Hence, in this space tourism leisure industry, it does not ensure that the rich or high income people must be persuade to choose this kind of expensive space tourism entertainment in whose holiday or retirement time. They can have the common tourism entertainment to go to different countries to travel many times in our earth. Otherwise, space tourism leisure is more expensive to compare common earth tourism leisure , it means that the rich or high income people only spend one time spacecraft catching to fly to space to travel in their life, it is more difficult to every space traveler like to catch spacecraft to fly to space to travel more than one time, due to he/she had attempted to catch spacecraft to fly to space to travel to own space travel experience, he/she will feel enough satisfactory and enjoyment in common. Hence, it is possible that future many rich or high income people only like to spend one time space tourism leisure, then they won't continue to spend this kind of tourism entertainment again in their life.

Thus, space tourism leisure providers need to arrange any special or attractive space tourism leisure to persuade these high income or rich target clients to consume, when the economic environment will change worse. The Europen space agency (ESA), defines this phenomenon between economic environment variable and space tourism client growth or falling number relationship as: " space tourism is an execution of sub-orbital flight by privately finded and/or privately operated vehicles and the technology development driven by space tourism market."

it seems that space vehicle is one attractive travelling desire tool will be one attractive selling point to influence space tourism leisure consumer individual entertainment choice or attitude to be changed to positive leisure consumption attitude to prefer to play this kind of space tourism activities when economic environment changes to worse. Hence, when economic environment is worse, the economic wore changing factor will influence the space travelling planner individual leisure consumption desire, even it will influence the rich or high income young people or rich retirement people target customer both groups.

As (ESA, 2008) indicated space vehicle will be one kind of attractive leisure tool for spce traveler. So, I suggest that space tourism lesiure journey arrangement needs to include that such as : the space travelers can catch space vehicle to move on Moon or Mars plants land to feel what the different feeling is between during they are catching public transportation tool, such as bus or taxi during the are catching these transportation tools on earth land and during they are catching space vehicle tools on Mars or Moon planet's lands. It is so exciting and fun catching space vehicle tool experience on these both Mars or Moon planets' lands to the young and old age space travelling passengers. Because every space vehicle's speed is not very fast and it will move on Moon or Mars planets slowly. So, any aged pace travelling passengers can attempt to play this kind of space facilities leisure after they catched spacecraft to fly to these both Mars or Moon planet to stay. They can spend half hour or one hour, even more than one hour to catch the space vehicle to go to anywhere on Mars or Moon to travel. It is possible that they can find exciting and undiscovered things on these both planets.

So, catching space vehicle to go to anywhere on either these both planets journey, it will one essential part of space travelling journey during the economic environment is changed to worse. It is extra attractive space travelling leisure journey to attract space tourism consumer individual leisure desire when economic environment is worse.

Hence, from this perspective then space tourism could be understood as a section of the tourism industry mainly based on technological development, progression and its activity being related specifically to sub orbital flights. So, if future space tourism providers expect whether the global economic environment changing will be better or worse which won't influence space tourism leisure consumption desire to be changed. The space tourism leisure providers need to persuade the space tourism planners feel space tourism would have to be treated like an already exciting part of the tourism industry. It means that space tourism leisure is one kind of tourism leisure choice to replace common earth tourism leisure consumption. When travelers feel space tourism is another tourism leisure to replace which can replace common earth tourism leisure. It will avoid the worse economic environment changing factor to reduce the rich or high income young people or rich retirement old people whose space travelling leisure consumption desire.

Consequently , the question in relation to, in what kinds of space tourism journey message do space travel providers promote behind whether space vehicle journey promotion message which is needed when economic environment will change worse. I shall be asked, as understanding the meaning in which space tourism is being marketed, communicated is seen as a factor , which can either positively contribute to future development of the tourism industry or lead into prolonging or seen stopping the space tourism industry from its progression.

(2) Space tourism leisure journey management factor

Secondly, space tourism leisure jounrey management factor, how to arrange every space tourism leisure journey which will be one important factor to influence space tourism planner individual tourism consumption desire.

In general, it can includes these several forms of space tourism leisure activities in every space lesiure trip arrangement. The following classification of space tourism include: Terrestria spce tourism (i.e. NASA visit centre, space movies, online space experience); Atmospheric space tourism (i.e. : MIG 31 flight, zero G. flights) and astro (orbita) tourism (i.e.: trips to the international space station-beyond earth orbit) (Cater 2010, Crouch et al. 2009).

Instead of US domestic space tourism market is potential, next country is Japan. First, the study is made by Collins et. al (1994, 1996) in Japan on 3030 research participants, showed that 80% of respondents under the age of 50 were willing to travel to space and out of them 20% were willing to pay year's salary for the space travel experience. Yet, it could be citicized that the Japan people age group of under 50 could be too broad, in general different generations under one groups. nest besides the willingness to go to space, the Japanese study showed respondents motivations for travelling to space, including any fun and exciting attractive space tourism journey, e.g. interest in space walk, catching space vehicle or driving space vehicle on the either Moon or Mars planets, earth view, zeo gravity experience, livin gin space hotels one night or more, watching movies in space cinemas, swimming in space pools, visiting space gardens, running in space sport centers, catching spacecrafts to view earth or Moon or Mars planets.

Hence, it seems attractive space tourism journey can persuade another country's space travelling planners, such as Japanese attempts to satisfy whose space tourism needs. So, different kinds of attractive space trip journey arrangement will be one important factor to influence young and old age travelling consumption desire. It implies that attractive space tourism journey will be one influential factor to encourage other countries tourism consumers attempt to another kind of leaving earth tourism leisure. So, any space tourism trip destinations and leisure facilities arrangement must need to satisfy space traveler individual leisure needs and every space trip must be more fun, exciting and comfortable and enjoyable feeling to compare general tourism journey in earth. Due to general earth tourism leisure will be space tourism leisure's competitive or replaced leisure product and service. Hence, space trip destinations and leisure facilities choice will be one important factor to influence space travelling planner's consumption desire.

Every space travelling planner will compare general earth travelling leisure's destinations and leisure facilities arrangement whether the space travelling trip arrangement , leisure facilities arrangement and food arrangement, space vehicle or spacecraf leisure comfortable influence issues which will have more satisfactory enjoyable feeling to compare general earth tourism leisure and their spending expenditure to every space trip whether is value or is not value.

Consequently, economic environment changing factor and space trip and leisure facilities arrangement factor which both will influence any space tourism planner individual consumption desire mainly. So, space tourism businessmen ought concern these two aspects of factors how and when will change to adapt any country's potential space traveler's space tourism changing taste and needs in order to follow the new space tourism changing needs easily.

Space tourism market moral ethic risk threats

What are space tourism moral ethic risk during the space businessmen operate this businesses as well as what market threats who will encounter to face difficulties ? I shall give actul cases to explain how and why these challenges will cause to influence any new space tourism businesses development successfully.

(1) Potential accidents aspect

Firstly, space travelers will concern that public reactions to potential accidents aspect during they are catching spacecrafts to travel to space. In fact, it is moral ethic responsibility to any space tourism leisure providers to provide safe, comfortable and non accident occurrence in their whole space trip. Because once time accident will cause any one of space passenger hurt or death. So , it must be any space tourism businessmen responsibilities to concern whether they have enough confidence to ensure none any accident occurrences in every space tourism trip.

Hence, in space tourism industry, government needs have public policy to threaten or prohibit any space tourism leisure providers neglect to often check and ensure any spacecraft machines or equipments are regular opeations, as well as often renew new spacecraft machines when they are old to be used. The policy is a force effort to need them to abide every space tourism leisure safe responsibility to ensure or guarantee any one of spacecraft won't have accident occurrences during it has left earth to fly to space in whole space trip journey from the beginning to the end till to the spacecraft come to earth safely.

Hence, this policy forces any space tourism leisure providers concern to put a monetary value on increased or reduced risk of death, the " value of statistical live", used to characterize when the benefit of safety regulation is worth the cost such regulation improves. So, the country government and the country's space tourism leisure providers both have responsibilities to guarantee all space tourism passengers' life safety. It must not allow any death or hurt occurrences during every space tourism trip.

Even, the country government can have legal action to publish any space tourism leisure providers, when their every space tourism trip has occurred accidents, e.g. fire accident occurrence in spacecarft or spacecrat machines are broken to be damaged and need to be repaired during the space tourism trip. It will threaten to reduce trip accident occurrence, such as this cases. The commercial space ventures may present risk to property as well, such as a fire starting on the ground by launch-related material or problems presented by space debris.

In principle, liability law can provide incentive to deter carelessness that could lead to the destruction of property, although statutory (rather than common law) assignments of liability for commercial launches are somewhat problematic.

Consequently, if the space tourism leisure provider expected to grow space tourism passenger number in long -term time, it must need to ensure none any accidents can occur during any space trip. Otherwise, the space tourism passengers can choose another space tourism leisure provider to replace its spce tourism leisure easily.

(2) Space tourism destinations and space tourism entertainment facilities safe arrangement challenges aspect

Secondly, it is space tourism destinations and space tourism entertainment facilities safe arrangement challenges. Nowadays, commercial space travel is looking more like a real possibility than science fiction. The usual ethical issues related to the safety of the space destination choices and the space tourism entertainment facilities, e.g. space vehicles, space hotels, space swimming pools, space sport centers, space cinemas, space gardens, space farming lands. In this strange space environment and safety concerns are just the beginning as there are othe interesting questions, such as below:

What likely would be a fair process for commercializing or claiming property in any space planets? Such as Moon or mars, when any future space tourism leisure providers who need to build above these any one of space entertainment facilities on these planets to provide to their space travelling customers to play.

How to distribute and manage these any lands ownership to these future space tourism providers fairly and legally?

How likely would a separatist movement be among space settlements to want to be free and independent states?

How to ensure above future space entertainment facilities and space entertainment places are in the safe space environment to be provided to any space travelers to play in any planets, e.g. Moon or Mars etc. planets.

So, concerning how to arrange space entertainment facilities to provide to space tourism clients to play in any safe space environment issue, it will be another concerning question to every space tourism leisure providers. When they decide to choose anywhere to the space hotels, space swimming pools, space gardens, space cinemas or space farming lands or space sport centers. These space buildings will need to be built in the safe, on stable stone lands environment and none any natural distaster, such as large wind or space underground water etc. unpredictable space natural distasterr attack to these space buildings suddenly. Because it has responsibility to any space tourism leisure providers to guarantee any one of these space buildings are safe to be built in the planet's safe land environment. It aims to achieve none any accident occurrences during their space tourism clients are staying to enter these any one of space buildings to visit or play any space entertainment facilities safely, e.g. space vehicle.

So, they must need to ceck anywhere the space planet's places to be ensured safe to build any buildings. Then, they can choose the suitable locations to build space entertainment facilities or buildings more confidently.

In fact, any space entertainment facilities, e.g. space hotels, space farming lands as well as space transportation tools, e.g. spce vehicle, spacecraft , these things will be value to be concerned to any space tourism leisure providers and it is business moral ethic responsibility to every one of them, when they plan to develop their space tourism business in any planets.

(3) Space tourism market competition challenge aspect

Thirdly, any provate space tourism development leisure businesses will face market competitive challenge, such as large spacefaring countries, e.g. US, UK have possible to dominate future space tourism leisure business (government can own space tourism leisure business). They will be main actors in space were nation-states. Large spacefaring counties can build the space vehicles, that can take people and cargo into orbit and to the Moon, or Mars crafted international space law and shaped the main investments in space tourism leisure technology.

So, it is possible that the own space technological developed countries, such as US, UK, these countries governemts will have possible to operate public fund to support space tourism leisure business. It implies that private space tourism leisure businesses will face public space tourism leisure business and themselve private space tourism leisure business market competition in space tourism leisure industry.

If these two countries governments also participate this private space tourism leisure market. It will raise market threats to any private space tourism organizations.

Whether will developed countries governments participate private space tourism market? It is possible that new commercial actors began to enter the space tourism leisure industry, looking to disrupt both space launch services ans use space in new exotic ways. For example, the US government also moved its purposeful degradatoin of the global positioning system (GPS), so US government will have effort to dominate GPS global positioning system communication business also. As this GPS communication business case, future US government has possible to decide to participate space tourism leisure business also.

However, in the future, space tourism leisure industry may contribute even more the developed countries, e.g. American, England economy. Space tourism and resource recovery, e.g. mining on planet, Moons and asteroids in particular may become large parts of that space tourism industry if these countries governments participated to this space tourism industry development. Of course, their viability rests on a range of factors, including costs , future regulation, international market competivitive problems and assumption about space technological development. However, these is increasing optimism in these areas of economic production to bring human space tourism leisure enjoyment and space mining resource development benefits. But the space economy is not just about what happens in orbits or how that alters life on the ground. The growth of this economy can also contribite to new innovations across all future possible unpredictable or undiscovered technological development, instead of space tourism leisure or space mining resource exploitation development.

Consequently, any space development technological governments will have possible to bring economic benefits from either only private space tourism leisure organizations or governments and private space tourism leisure both organizations cooperate to participate to achieve space tourism misson to contribute to global economic development and create new jobs to be employed in space labor supply market.

● Can space tourism business bring
economy benefits

It is fact that space tourism activities have a positive and beneficial impact on eveyday life and society and this help space travelers to understand that, despite the high space ticket prices of any space tourism leisure choices. However, space tourism will bring scientific knowledge and technological knowhow and jobs to bring humn tangible or untangible both benefits. I shall indicate these benefits as below:

Although, space tourism leisure seems only leisure activities to be consumed to satisfy any space tourism individual travelling need. However, it can assign space scientists to research and attempt discovery these intangible benefits: Such as tele-communications revolution, satellite weather forecasting, mapping mineral exploration, water resource management diaster mitigation, national security or other undiscovered untangible benefits. Because every spacecraft needs to plan to fly to space, and it will reach any space planet stations, e.g. Mars, Moon planet when it visits these any one planet, the space scientists can attempt to find new undiscovered space resource , e.g. mining or finding new undiscovered satellite weather forecasting method when they can reach these planets to attempt to do space scientifical investigtion to research new space resource , or find any space stones attack to our methods to avoid earth disaster occurrence (national security mission), instead of the spacecraft catchs space passengers to visit these planets to enjoy these planets space entertainment facilities in their space trip journeys.

(1) On space resource benefit aspect

Hence, the space tourism intangible benefits include: space exploration and international cooperation is developing sophisticted space technologies by nations. For example, the images of distant stars and glaxies using Hubble telescope, research laboratory such as international space station to conduct experiments in biology, human biology, physics, Astronomy and meteorology under microgravity environment and testing of the spacecraft systems will be required for space tourism missions to the Moon and Mars. In the future, human would be able to have unlimited and clean solar energy from space for our industries as well as heating and lighting our homes. In the near future , it would be possible to disposed-off our nuclear waste safely and unexpensively and released towards the sun using a space elevator. We many become a space tourist in earth orbit or on the Moon or Mars. We may carry and extra-terrestial mining and even introduce the development of a multi-planet economy.

(2) On education benefit aspect

Another on education benefit aspect, space tourism can let space travelers to feel actual space learning experiences, during the spacecraft is flying in the space. Their space environment learning experience can include, for example: How many spacecraft have been launched by a given country? How many phone calls are made over a satellite? How many lives could be saved by resue satellites? How they feel differences when they are living in one space hotels, they are swimming in the swimming pools, they are visiting the space garden, they are running in one space sport centers, they are visiting in one space farming land, they are sitting or driving one space vehicle on planet land, or they are catching one spacecraft.

These space learning experience will let they feel what the actual differences between space environment and earth environment. It is one humankind learning experience education service in any space planet's Moon or Mars remote areas, bringing information and tourism entertainment facilities to the masses. The space experience learning knowledge can provide data to let these space travelers to know, such as how ships can be safe at sea, monitoring the threat of pollution, how enhancing durable medical instruments for better health-care enabling hikers and skiers to be located when lost, many more. So, it seems space tourism can bring much positive benefits as no negative impact on space activitied has been found by the society , the investments are made by the nations on space activites are justified and not the waste of money.

● What are the tangible social and economic benefits brought from space tourism?

In most advanced economies space tourism or space resource exploitation industry is seen as an enabler that improves lives and helps to develop both economic and social spheres. Space industry economic can include these aspect: Application of space technology to space tourism navigation, meteorological forcasting and broadcast of on live television and internet connectivity to lesser-known applications, such as precision agriculture, transport, tracking, resource extraction and monitoring of utility networks.

Additional application exists in the disaster monitoring and relif, insurance and military applications. Thus, data coming from satellites is important to all economic sectors, making the world a better and safer place.

International space tourism experience would suggest that space travelling leisure businesses deliver value by providing a central point for academia industry , defence and foreign entities to collaborate among themselves and with government and to facilitate the flow of knowledge and capital.

How can space tourism industry maximize the socio-economic benefits? In fact, our growing use of space derived data and systems is our growing dependence on a better and safer sapce planet, e.g. Moon or Mars and to provide space tourism safe services that space travelling service that space traveler all benefit from industry in telecommunication , health, transport , banking , security and climate change monitoring.

The space tourism positive influence result is long term, the positive contribution to our quality of life is real. In other word, the world for space tourism leisure activities is changing the internationally space tourism sector is experiencing a profound revolution.

In conclusion, space tourism leisure countries with historical leadership in space tourism have been under positive as a result of a tough financial environment leading to the definition of their space travelling technology priorities. In the meantime, new space entertainment travelling leaders, such as US, UK , even China, India have ambitions in space tourism through massive investments in the development of their capabilities in space travelling leisure business aspect.

So, the future space travelling entertainment market is large, due to China and India both have many rich people and high income people, who expect to consume in space tourism leisure trip at least one time in their lifes. Consequently, worldwide space tourism entertainment industry players are rethinking their busines models and strategies as they experience discuptive innovations, competitive space tourism entertainment and new drivers impacting the spacecraft and any space entertainment facilities manufacturing on Moon or Mars planet, launch and space tourism entertainment related businesses. Thus, we can in fact in talk about a new space tourism business, in which more and more innovative applications of space tourism data are developed dependence on space tourism data in everyday life rises and increasing share of economic growth relies on the space tourism market both in terms of opportunity benefits , e.g. India and China spce tourism potential market development and any concern space tourism job creation to every countries. Hence, space tourism development can bring positive economic benefits to any countries.

Space flight safe factor

To operate one space flight exploration organization, it needs to concern human safe flight factor. I shall indicate it needs to have these three stages to further develop its space exploration to continue to improve its safe space flight for every time of space flight.

Human future space flight missions will include these three stages to continue journey into space. The first stage is short term, NASA's return to flight after the Columbia accident. The second stage is mid term. What is needed to continue flying the shuttle fleet until a replacement means for human access to space and for other shuttle capabilities is available, and the third stage is long term, future directions for the kinds in space. Therefore, the space exploration organization can arrange the three stages to carry out any future space exploration activities. I believe it can improve every time of space flight more safe because it can ensure its space rocket engineering can be improved to raise safe level to let space people to catch to leave our Earth.

However, any human future space flight, which must be enhanced safety of flight when carry on any experimenting space flight exploration missions. Because NASA's safety performance is a very important factor to influence any space people confidence to catch every sky rocket to leave our Earth to do any space exploration activities. So, eliminating and catching rocket risks will be any beginning and end than during the middle of any space flight exploration journeys.

Space people's life is the most important assets of any space exploration journeys. Because of the dangers of ascent and re-entry, because of unknown space environment and because we are still relative new comers, operation of shuttle and indeed all human space flight must be viewed as a development activity.

Thus, any every time space flight exploration missions will need to encourage to invent new space transportation engines (machine) or fuel, e.g. nuclear fuel to reduce the any space exploration journey accident risks and achieves to spend the fastest time to arrive any new space exploration destination. Thus, I believe any new space exploration flight will improve the space transportation technology and invent more new fuel and new space rocket manufacturing materials for future human any unknown space exploration flight demand. The three stages of improving space transportation include as below:

The beginning stage, for example, the space shuttle is as somehow comparable to civil or military air transport. They are not comparable; the inherent risks of spaceflight are serious higher. The recognition of human spaceflight as a developmental activity requires a shift in focus from operations and meeting schedules to a concern for the risks involves. Thus, the space transportation tools will be improved to protect space passengers safety: the improving the ability to tolerate it, repairing the damage on a timely basis, reducing unforeseen events from the loss of crew and vehicle, exploring all options for survival, such as provisions for crew escape systems and safe havens , barring unwarranted departures from design standards and adjusting standards only under the most safety-driven process.

The mid-term stage, the present shuttle is not very safe to fly in space. Thus, focus on safe return to flight is very important to every space flight journey rules , they leave Earth and arrive any another new planet destination, then come back our Earth again in every space exploration journey (flight). Thus, the energy will be space transportation tool one important factor. If the space transportation tool has enough supply, which won't stay in space and can not fly in space suddenly. Thus, the every time of the human space flight will be taken more time and effort then would be reasonable to expect prior to return to flight. Thus, human space exploration organization needs have higher reliability organization structure to manage every space flight, e.g. one is separating technical authority from the function of managing schedules and cost. Another is an independent safety and mission assurance organization.

It is the capability for effective systems integration perhaps even more challenging than these organizational changes are the cultural changes requires. Thus, the cultural to safe and effective space rocket operations are real and substantial. If the space exploration organization has good culture to let every staffs can communicate easily. I believe the every time space exploration accident will be reduced. Examples include: the tendency to keep knowledge of problems contained within a center or program, technical decisions, without in -depth, peer-reviewed technical analysis, and an unofficial hierarchy or system created by placing excessive power in one office. Such factors interfere with open communication, the shared of lesson learned, cause duplication and expenditure of resources and create a burden for managers to reduce undesirable characteristics threaten safety.

Thus, any space exploration trip, rocket equipment safety and check are very important factor to prepare for every time space flight. The reason is that space flight must guarantee any space people who can come back Earth, if the rocket equipment are poor and lack maintenance. The, the space people whose life is dangerous. Due any space exploration organization mission require human presence in space. For example, president John Kennedy's 1961 charge to send Americans to the moon and return then safely to Earth. Thus, the space exploration organization has attempted to carry out a similar high priority mission that would justify the expenditure of resources on a scale equivalent to those allocated for project Apollo. Also, the space exploration organization has had to participate in the give and take of the normal political process in order to obtain the resources needed to carry out its programs.

Another main successful factor in the final stage, the space exploration organization needs have a clearly defined long term space mission to commit over the past decade to improve future space exploration flight safety by developing a second generation space transportation system. So, for long term, the space exploration organization should need to plan for future space transportation capabilities without making them dependent on technological breakthroughs.

For example, mission for a post Apollo effort that involved full development of low-Earth orbit, permanent outposts on the moon, and initial journeys to Mars planet. Since that rejection, these objective, have reappeared as central elements in many proposals, setting a long term vision for any space exploration flight programs in the future.

Thus, space organization future space exploration mission for 21 St century is to lead the exploration and development of the space frontier, advance science, technology and enterprise and building institutions and systems that make accessible vast new resources and support human settlements beyond Earth orbit from the highland of the Moon to the plains of Mars. Thus, the space exploration organization limit is to conduct the research required to plan missions to Mars and/or other distant destinations. This is the most safe space flight distance limit by the space rocket equipment, machine installation , quality and effort to guarantee space people life safety when who catch the space rocket life safety when who catch the rocket to leave Earth to arrive any space destination in any space flight. However, human travel to destinations beyond Earth orbit has not been adopted because it is too far space flight to cause accident risk. Hence, space exploration organization future invention of long term need is that the role of new space transportation capabilities in enabling whatever space goals need to choose to pursue for human present in Earth orbit vision.

In conclusion, space exploration organization needs to in-depth examination space shuttle safe issue, how to reach an inescapable design of the space shuttle, because that the design was based in many aspects on how absolute technologies and because the space shutter is now an aging system , but still developmental in character, it is in the space organization is interest to replace the shuttle as soon as possible as the primary aim for transporting humans to and from Earth orbit.

● How to develop new economic tourism industry after COVID 19 disease disappears ?

How to develop tourism industry in new economic environment? Any examination of the new economic development of travel and tourism requires definitions of the subject and its components, which are suitable for economic analysis. However, in new economic development to tourism industry, it is also important to look at tourism conceptually, in order to set the scene for a deeper understanding of the future new tourism industry development.

Tourism is neither a phenomenon nor a simple set if industries, however, in new or old economic development environment. It is a human activity which encompasses human behavior, use of resources, and interaction with other people, economies and leisure enjoyment environment. It is also involved physical movement of tourists to locales other than their normal living places.

In future new economic environment, traditional travel needs to include these element in order to satisfy traveler enjoyment and leisure feeling: They may include: Tourist needs and motivations, tourism selection and behavior and constraints , travel away from home , market interactions between tourists and those supplying products to satisfy tourist needs and impacts on tourists , hosts, economies and environments.

In new economic environment, the tourism products may include: carriers, in any forms of transport for tourist travel accommodation, man-made attractions, which could also include the managed areas of natural attractions, private sector and public sector support services, middlemen, such as tour wholesalers and travel agents.

The tourism resources may also include: Natural resources, lands , minerals, water and biological; labor resources, human work, and enterprise; capital resources, manmade enhancement and other resources. The travel and tourism resources problems may include: As there is frequently a mismatch between producer and consumer perception of what constitutes the tourism product , there may be conflict in ideas of which resources are properly involved as well as many of the resources likely to be in demand for tourism are public goods , or even free resources.

In new economic development to tourism industry view, we need to consider that tourism and travel has the reputation of being a relatively clean and pleasant industry in which to work or invest in order to attract a greater number of resource suppliers than as less well-perceived industry, which therefore keeps rewards prices down by competition, how to attract those retiring from or travel business for example, if their finances are already sound, income from travel is not expected to be optimal , travel and tourism is frequently highly seasonal , offering rewards that are competitive with other industries only some of the time, destination products are often in locations which are of little use to other industries, so that competition for resource use if minimal and hence rewards are low.

In general, tourist purpose may include: recreational purpose : holiday, health and sport and religion as well as business purpose: company business

, e.g. conventions and sales trips. So, in new economic tourism development aim, tourism industry need consider hoe to achieve incentive trips to let these both tourists to feel. For example, the overall type of tourism required, destination arrangement, travel mode, accommodation and attraction visiting and purchasing method or distribution channel. The purchasing method choices may include: whether to buy an inclusive package or separate service, whether to buy direct from suppliers, such as airlines or hotels or use an agent , which tour wholesaler or operate or agent to use.

I predict the tourism development in new economic view, it may have these characteristics: Few enterprises in travel and tourism are large, highly cashed-up and have a large asset base, enterprises within travel and tourism that are not in a financial position to diversify, and those do well success to the above –average growth obtainable in travel and tourism compared with many other industries, they would therefore tend to expand within the sector. The result of individual enterprise growth and integration within travel and tourism is an increase in the concentration of that industry. The degree to which output is produced of fewer and fewer enterprises. This can be only be accounted for realistically with the context of an individual economy, Levels of concentration in any part of travel and tourism in the future are likely to depend on two opposing factors: The constant demand by many tourist market segments for new experiences and products, which encourages the development and survival of more and diverse enterprises, and therefore leads to the reduction of concentration as well as technology, which in travel and tourism frequently calls for large capital outlays and requires mass markets for efficient use, promotes integrations and large scale enterprise, especially in air travel and non-personal services (marketing and information communication, travel insurance , tourism payment methods). IN these areas, concentration will undoubtedly increase in future new economic development environment.

● How new economic development in oil industry after COIV 19 disease

The future global economic growth, it will influence personal incomes and GDP rise. They would carry different weight in different countries at different times. Starting from low levels of incomer and economic development. Household consumption will change from being dominated by basic heat to rapidly rising energy use for higher levels of comfort in space heating and cooling (and large dwellings), and greater use of electrical appliances, finally to a degree of saturation influenced by the income distribution patterns of the country concerned. Income distribution typically changes very slowly, so that the technical market for heart will never be saturated because there will always be a proportion of poor people living in small spaces less comfortably than the average. Industrial energy consumption will be influenced by technical efficiency within each sector, and by changes in the structures of the economy, e.g. changing proportions of agriculture, heavy and light industry, and services. One may eventually see evidence of diminishing marginal returns to additional energy inputs compared to other inputs. Energy consumption in the energy transformation sector may be influenced by income, which drives the demand for electricity to influenced by income, which drives the demand for electricity to grow faster than the demand for heat, but is also subject to the chosen technology of transformation, which is influenced by the cost and availability of primary energy inputs (fuels) in new economic development environment.

IN new economic development environment, it will influences that fuels do not compete in all sectors; for example, the transport sector is dominated by oil. Nuclear and hydroelectric power (and most renewables) reach the user through electricity; electricity itself competes with the direct burning of fossil fuels. Electricity provides the means by which other fuels can compete with oil and gas in sectors, such as space heating and process heat. It also is the only means of powering applications such as motors, computers and lighting: these subsectors are difficult to analyze. However, there is strong evidence that higher incomes do not weaken the demand for electricity so much as the demand for energy in total (in contrast to the effect on the demand for non-electric energy forms).

Econometricians look at the historical record of change in fuel prices and quantities to distinguish several factors between the new economic development and old economic development to oil industry in the future. An income effect. Increasing (reducing) fuel prices reduces (increases) the purchasing power of consumers' income: higher incomes caused by lower prices will increase energy consumption; the consumers' allocation of the increased income to energy purchases may reduce as income rises. Thus income may be heading in a different direction from fuel prices that the effect of fuel price changes when incomes are rising means simply that rising incomes have increased demand. Reducing the cost of using energy through win-win efficiency measures causes a similar problem . On the consequence, in future new economic development environment, it may influence in both cases demand will be less than if the future oil price or efficiency has not changed. The other effect is that an efficiency or substitution effect. An increase in fuel prices may cause consumers to spend more on new equipment, building materials and management operations, which will reduce the amount of fuel required to give the same energy result to the user. The extent of the efficiency effect depends on what happens to the price of the new equipment or building: if those price s rise in line with the fuel price, changes in the balances between fuel and capital or management will not occur. A new user technology , such as the development of the combined cycle gas turbine generator may increase efficiency and thus greatly reduce the quantity of primary fuel needed to produce the required output in this case electricity. If electricity prices had remained sticky, and the electricity and gas markets were not competitive, some of this advantages could have accrued to the gas suppliers in the form of an increase in price, because th4 unit of gas produces more output of electricity, it would have a higher value. In reality, the development of new economic competitive environment in both gas and electricity has tended to ensure that the benefits of such technical advanced accrue to the consumer through lower final prices. The same many apply in the case of improved efficiency in future non-manual driving auto vehicle development: the consumer's cost of motoring is reduced in new economic non-manual driven auto vehicle (Artificial intelligent vehicle) can replace manual driven vehicle , even electricity battery can replace oil energy to be used in vehicles. So, oil price may be influenced to reduce in future new economic development environment.

COVID 19 disease how brings online shopping behavior chance

The huge rise in digital commerce, especially among new or low-frequency consumers, is likely to continue post-pandemic.Nowadays, COVID 19 disease had influence global visiting shop consumers choose to buy any products from online. I shall indicate US online shopping development trend example as below:

Months into the coronavirus disease 2019 (COVID-19) pandemic, Americans' online shopping habits are continuing to shift. We documented changes in online shopping habits at the beginning of the pandemic, comparing patterns from January and February (before the pandemic) with patterns from mid-March and April (when lockdowns and other restrictions were beginning).

We now present findings from an August 2020 RAND American Life Panel (ALP) survey, in which we followed up with approximately 1,900 of our original respondents. In this survey, we asked respondents how often they shopped online in July and August. This survey reflects not only how often people are shopping online and whether they are spending more or less on online shopping, but how shopping behaviors have (or have not) changed since the early days of the COVID-19 pandemic.

We have divided our respondents into three categories on the basis of how often they shop online: frequent (once a week or more), occasional (a few times a month) and infrequent (never or almost never) online shoppers.

In January and February, our respondents were roughly equally split between these categories, as Figure 1 shows. This pattern changed substantially: Online shopping became more common as COVID-19 spread. This change has persisted as the pandemic continues. By August, about 45 percent of our respondents were frequent, one-third were occasional, and only one-quarter were infrequent online shoppers.

By summer 2020, overall trends in online shopping had substantially changed, although these changes were by no means universal. The frequency of online shopping has continued to increase; frequent online shoppers have risen from 35 to 45 percent of all shoppers, even as 55 percent of respondents stuck with their prepandemic habits. Forty percent of our respondents were spending more money online, even as 20 percent were spending less. These trends reinforce what other data show: Although many households have been able to pivot to working and shopping from home, some of those in less-fortunate circumstances are cutting back.

In the August ALP survey, also asked respondents to estimate whether the amount of money that they had spent on online purchases had gone up or down since February. Specifically, we asked respondents whether their spending had doubled, increased by a smaller amount, stayed about the same, or decreased. We cannot calculate exactly how much more or less households are spending, but these responses do provide some sense of changes at the household level.

Thirty-nine percent of Americans reported that they had increased their online spending—11 percent estimated that they had doubled their spending and 28 percent estimated that they had increased it by a smaller amount. Forty-three percent reported spending about the same amount of money, and 19 percent reported spending less.

Unsurprisingly, people who said that they shopped online more frequently were generally spending more on online purchases, although the pattern is not clear-cut. Of those who were shopping online more in July and August, about half were also spending more money. About 42 percent said that their spending had not changed, and 9 percent said that it actually had decreased. Among people who were doing the same amount of online shopping or were shopping online less often, 32 to 35 percent were spending more and about 25 percent were spending less. (ALP surveys, Mayn and Aug. 2020).

SOURCE: Authors' calculations using 1,883 responses in the ALP surveys that were conducted in May and August 2020.

NOTE: Respondents were asked the following question: "Over the past month, how often did you do online shopping or get home delivery of any products, including meals, groceries, medication, clothing, books, or other products?" Responses are weighted using sampling weights, as described in Carman and Nataraj, 2020.

Thus, it implies that COVD 19 disease had influenced many US consumers choose to buy any products from online. US Household income seems to be related to spending on online shopping, although perhaps not in the expected direction. Households earning less than $40,000 were more likely to decrease their online spending than higher-income households since March, but they were also most likely to double their online spending within the same time period. It is possible that these households are still spending less in total dollar value than other households, even if they have doubled their spending.

Bibliography

Carman, Katherine Grace, and Shanthi Nataraj, 2020 American Life Panel Survey on Impacts of COVID-19: Technical Documentation, Santa Monica, Calif.: RAND Corporation, RR-A308-1, 2020. As of November 2, 2020: https://www.rand.org/pubs/research_reports/RRA308-1.html

———, 2020 American Life Panel Survey on Impacts of COVID-19: May 2020 Survey Results, Santa Monica, Calif.: RAND Corporation, RR-A308-2-v2, 2020. As of November 2, 2020: https://www.rand.org/pubs/research_reports/RRA308-1.html

———, 2020 American Life Panel Survey on Impacts of COVID-19: August

2020 Survey Results, Santa Monica, Calif.: RAND Corporation, RR-A308-8, 2020. As of November 2, 2020: https://www.rand.org/pubs/ research_reports/RRA308-1.html
Cohen, Patricia, Ben Casselman, and Gillian Friedman, "An Extra $600 a Week Kept Many Jobless Workers Afloat. Now What Will They Do?" New York Times, July 29, 2020, updated September 10, 2020.

Thus, COVID 19 disease had influene the global buying habits of shoppers tend to change slowly. Covid-19, however, has been disruptive enough to shake them up, and companies are trying to take advantage.

global businesses need to bring all creatures of habit, and shopping is largely habit-driven. There are very few times in one's life when you have an opportunity to reshape their habits. The classic three are when you get married, when you move home and when you have a baby. And otherwise, your habits are pretty cemented, and you're not really open to forming new habits. And so what this current moment has created is a moment when everyone's habits are up for grabs.

What Is the Risk of Getting COVID-19 While Shopping in order to bring online shopping chance raises?

Whether the shopping is indoors or outdoors, with outdoors being safer the number of people shopping — fewer means it's easier to maintain social (physical) distancing how long you'll take — the faster you're done, the better COVID-19 positivity rate in the local community. So, global many consumers had felt online shopping is more safe to compare to visit shops by COVID 19 disease influence.

The impact of online grocery shopping on food consumer behavior in Covid-19. Some researchers Uses bivariate probit models to empirically investigate the impact of online purchasing channels on Chinese urban consumer food hoarding behaviors with random survey samples. Some research results show that fresh food e-commerce channels are more likely to be associated with panic stockpile behaviors due to higher likelihood of supply shortages than offline channels with government assistance in logistic management. In contrast, community group buy, another format of e-commerce, appears superior in satisfying the consumer needs and easing the panic buying perception.

It suggests that online channels may have diverse impacts on consumers' panic stockpiling behaviors during the extreme situations. Online channels need to develop efficient supply chains to be more resilient to extreme situations and the government shall recognize the increasing share of the online channels together with traditional offline channels when implementing supporting policies. With ever increasing share of online channels, it is imperative in terms of policy implications to understand how would online channels affect hoarding behavior.

Originality/value

They are the first study in online shopping's impact on food stockpile during pandemics using a random sample. Although food stockpile behavior at times of emergency have been investigated in many literature, there are no empirical studies on the impact of online channels on stockpile behaviors under extreme situations. Unlike disasters that immediately impact every entity in supply chains covering producers, vendors, distribution centers and retailers, pandemics did not render supply chains affected immediately, but rather increase consumers' willingness to shop online to avoid virus. Thus, Covid-19 provides a natural experiment to investigate the online channels' impact on stockpile behavior. So, COVID 19 disease may influence many consumers choose to buy foods from online channel. So, technology encourages supermarket food online shopping number increases when COVID illness occurs.

Source: Common Thread Collective

How online movie and online shopping online ebook online culture leisure activities technology encourages customers choice when COVID illness occurs ?

While ecommerce sales do not generally appear to be skyrocketing as one might expect, there are some exceptions. One of these is in subscription and convenience services, which have seen significant upward trends in both revenue and conversion.

Performance branding company WITHIN has been tracking the effects of COVID-19 on ecommerce across a number of specific sectors by monitoring and comparing data from select businesses year-over-year. This graph comes from their observations:

Impact of the COVID-19 pandemic on the arts and cultural heritage, entertainment and sport lesiure industry

The epidemic had a sudden and substantial impact on the arts and cultural heritage (GLAM) sectors worldwide. The global health crisis and the uncertainty resulting from it profoundly affected organisations' operations as well as individuals – both employed and independent – across the sector. By March 2020, across the world most cultural institutions had been indefinitely closed (or at least with their services radically curtailed) exhibitions, events and performances cancelled or postponed. Many individuals temporarily or permanently lost contracts or employment with varying degrees of warning and financial assistance available. Equally, financial stimulus from governments and charities for artists, have provided greatly differing levels of support, depending on the sector and the country. In countries such as Australia, where the arts contributed to about 6.4% of GDP, effects on individuals and the economy have been significant.

The impact of COVID 19 disease how influences global cinema entertainment industry

The pandemic has impacted the film industry. Across the world and to varying degrees, cinemas have been closed, festivals have been cancelled or postponed, and film releases have been moved to future dates. As cinemas closed, the global box office dropped by billions of dollars, while streaming became more popular and the stock of Netflix rose; the stock of film exhibitors dropped dramatically. Almost all blockbusters to be released after the March opening weekend were postponed or cancelled around the world, with film productions also halted. Massive losses in the industry have been predicted.

The impact of COVD 19 disease infuences to television and video game entetainment industry, they have similar consumer behavior , this disease excits many young and old age audiences choose to watch movies at homes and young age people choose to buy video game to play at homes.

The COVID-19 pandemic has shut down or delayed production of television programs in several countries.[citation needed] However, a joint report from Apptopia and Braze showed a 30.7% increase in streaming sessions worldwide on platforms such as Disney+, Netflix, and Hulu during the month of March.

The pandemic also affected the video game sector to a smaller degree. As the outbreak appeared in China first, supply chains affected the manufacturing and production of some video game consoles, delaying their releases and making current supplies scarcer. As the outbreak and pandemic spread, several keystone trade events, including E3 2020, were cancelled over concerns of further spread. The economic impact on the video game sector is not expected to be as large as in film or other entertainment sectors as much of the work in video game production can be decentralised and performed remotely, and products distributed digitally to consumers regardless of various national and regional lockdowns on businesses and services.

How CVID 19 disease influences publish industry, it influences many readers choose to read e-books from home computer, they do not like to visit book shops to buy books.

In light of the public health situation in which includes afflicted regions where retail sectors deemed non-essential have been ordered closed for the interim, Diamond Comic Distributors announced on 24 March 2020 a full suspension of distributing published material and related merchandise as 1 April 2020 until further notice. As Diamond has a near-monopoly on printed comic book distribution, this is described as an "extinction-level event" that threatens to drive the entire specialized comic book retail sector out of business with that one move. As a result, publishers like IDW Publishing and Dark Horse Comics have suspended publication of their periodicals while DC Comics is exploring distribution alternatives including an increased focus on online retail of digital material.

COVID 19 disease influences online shopping has more customers global. The pandemic has impacted the retail sector. Shopping centres around the world responded by reducing hours or closing down temporarily. As of 18 March 2020, the footfall to shopping centres fell by up to 30%, with significant impact in every continent.Additionally, product demand exceeded supply for many consumables, resulting in empty retail shelves.In Australia, the pandemic has provided a new opportunity for daigou shoppers to re-sell into the China market.

Some retailers have employed contactless home delivery or curbside pickup for items purchased through e-commerce sites.By April, retailers had started implementing "retail to go" models where consumers could pick up their orders. An estimated 40% of shoppers were shopping online and choosing to pick up in-store, a behavior that had suddenly doubled as compared to the previous year.

Small-scale farmers have been embracing digital technologies as a way to directly sell produce, and community-supported agriculture and direct-sell delivery systems are on the rise. For Amazon ecommerce example, it help Amazon increases many online consumers. Many traditional visiting shops consumers began to choose to apply internet channel to buy any products. In mid-April, Amazon confirmed that workers at over half of its

110 U.S. warehouses had been diagnosed with coronavirus.On 16 June, the United States Department of Commerce announced that retail sales for the month of May had seen an increase of 17.7% from April as states began to reopen and lift restrictions. According to CNBC, This marks the biggest one month jump in the history of retailing in the United States. Numbers for June reflected a 7.5 percent rise in sales. So, it causes many shops close, due to many visting shop customers began to accept to apply internet or online channel to buy any products to replace visiting shops purchase method.

Hence, instead of COVID 19 disease influences tourism recession, it also brings many shops close, but it creates new online purchase model to excite many traditional visiting shop purchase consumers began to choose online purchase model in retail aspect. But it also influences many restaurants close, because many people feel fear to go to restaurants to eat, due to food environment may be one most serious COVID 19 disease places. So, many people choose to buy food to cook at home, so, supermarkets may be one attractive place to let us to choose to buy food more safe to compare restaurants. Thus, COVID 19 disease may cause some kinds of businesses close , but it also bring new chance to some kinds of businesses. So, ecommerce shopping channel may encourage online shopping activities increase when COVID19 influences many people spend much to stay at homes.

Can artificial intelligence development to tourism industry
● Artificial intelligence will bring what benefits to
Influence traveler consumption behavior or raising
Travelling leisure desire?

Artificial intelligence will bring what benefits to influence traveler consumption behaviors or raising travelling leisure desire? It would be unreasonable not to analyze how artificial intelligence is affecting, such a big part of global economy. Especially, how it leads travel media to develop. We need to answer those questions , before we hope predict how artificial intelligence can bring advantages to influence travelers to raise travelers travelling leisure desires in long time. Which tends will shape the travel industry? What will customers demand in their journeys? Which business models will prevail ? What role of artificial intelligence to play in future tourism industry? What new opportunities and business models do the new technology block chain and artificial intelligence offer for the travel industry? How is artificial intelligence future impacting the travel industry

? The utilization of artificial intelligence will how raise tourism demand? Future artificial intelligence tourism development may help travel leisure benefits on these several aspects. They may include geographical elements choice, the tourist generating regions choice, the tourist destination regional choices and the transit route regions choice.

It is one exciting tourism service arrangement for travelers when artificial intelligence is participated to any travel agents' travelling leisure provision services. Artificial intelligence can help any travelling customers to arrange whole journey of a tourists, in these stages . In the before booking stage, (AI) journey service arrangement may include these from searching and being inspired stage to discovering and planning stage and booking stages. During booking, (AI) journey service arrangement may include booking and defining and improving stages. Finally, in the alter booking stage, (AI) journey arrangement service may include experiencing and reflecting and share , it is the tourist's leisure feeling after he/she had experienced the whole travel journey service arrangement. So, the (AI) 's whole tourism journey arrangement whether it is suitable to the tourist to let him/her to feel satisfactory ; or more satisfactory ; or the most satisfactory enjoyment feeling to his/her journey. It depends on how the (AI) judges the whole tourism journey service arrangement, e.g. reasonable price and comfortable accommodation choice for the business traveler of leisure travel in order to satisfy his/her accommodation choice. Because artificial intelligence is one complex computer machine, it ought may help any tourists to search accommodation information to search the most reasonable price and the most comfortable accommodation choice from social media to compare the tourist himself/herself accommodation search activity in order to get the most accurate accommodation choice and in order to satisfy the tourist's living need in his/her whole journey. So, future artificial intelligence is applied to tourism leisure service arrangement aspect. (AI) is this a goal oriented execution for any one tourist before he/she makes the final accommodation choice, tourism destination choice. It needs to help the tourist to execute his/her whole journey process, no matter how difficult this process may seem for humans.

● How (AI)helps tourism industry to reduce cost ?

In the future, robotics or artificial intelligence systems dominate the tourism industry, they may include chat bots, travel assistants, and service robots to any travel agents service providers. Their roles may include these several aspects to any travel agents service providers. They may include searching and being inspired, discovering , planning and booking , refining and improving, how excites the tourist experiencing to the journey service arrangement, reflecting and how raising his/her tourism leisure enjoyment feeling during the whole tourism journey from customer intelligence platform service.

However, future travel agent intermediaries as well as inventory providers will start to focus on their quality of offering and journey arrangement service. Thus, they invest comparable less in operational excellence, e.g. concentration of digital systems at the search and booking phase and robots at the experience phase of the customer journey is almost self-explanatory, journey searching, planning and booking via internet is nowadays the norm. This, these are no hybrid systems necessary. However, during the experience phase, in which the traveler leaves the realms of the digital world, physical interaction, which can only be delivered by robots, regains importance. Since char bots , travel assistants as well as service robots are all representatives of systems used at the travelling customer interface. However, supposing when the travelling agent decides to install (AI) systems, can not be explained by the trend of a rebound on customer journey experience. However, during the expert discussions, it was revealed that most of the tourism industry does not consider technology a core competency and often lack the capacities to self-develop and install such (A I) systems.

However, it may also seem that AI can impact automatization tasks to tourism industry, chat bots or service robots are typical representatives in which artificial intelligence is used to automate a task previously done by humans. This can be called the automatization effect. Nevertheless, automatization through (AI) systems should not be equated with other forms of technology utilization which are called automatization too. Nowadays, the automatization through self-serving terminals, whether at airports through self-check terminals or at hotels through self check in systems is quite common in the tourism service industry. However, in travel agents service industry sector, the (AI) systems process itself is not automated, but rather changed from the airport check in / out organizations to the travel agent journey arrangement customer service organizations. Artificial intelligence on the other side truly automates these process. So that neither a human at the airport or travel agent journey service arrangement organizations nor the travelling customer much do it.

A recent example are (AI) supermarkets , such as the " Amazon Go" store in which can artificial intelligence system, which can recognize persons and objects, tracks people and the objects which they put in their shopping-bad and automatically bills their purchases on the customers bank account (S t a r k ، 2 0 1 7) ·

Another similar system is imaginable at hotels and airports in which a face-recognition system recognizes the arrival of guests and automatically checks them in. JetBlue is already testing such a system a Boston airport (E n t i s ، 2 0 1 7) ·

However, how tourism organizations apply (AI) system can be employed to increase its competitive advantages, it means that either be achieved through differentiation, meaning delivery supervisor benefits to the consumer, or lower cost. If the robotic can help any tourists to choose the cheapest and the most comfortable apartment to let the tourist to live in his journey, such as recommender systems in the booking stage generate further benefits for consumers. The effect, however, is often related to automatization cost deduction, such as(AI)system can help the tourist whose the whole journey apartment cost reduction. Thus, one could assume that (AI)systems which automate tasks are mainly implemented to reduce apartments living cost for the tourist's whole journey. For example, chat bots can undoubtedly be used to replace sales and service staff at the tourist interface.

However, many companies use chat bots to expand their sales and service offerings instead, without reducing the respective staff. AirFrance-K C M uses its chat bots to sell its products and inform its customers about flight schedules via new channels, such as the face book messenger. This service is available 24 hours a day and seven days a week. This is mainly because chat bots are pure digital systems and can this practically scaled –up indefinitely (Kelly , 2016).

A simple example is that many hotels utilize robots as a marketing tool to attract guests than as a true mean to save costs, it nevertheless shows the feasibility of such as model. A simpler use case would be the utilization of a vacuum cleaning robot to automate the task of cleaning the floor. It would replace a share of the existing cleaning personal and this gave costs. However, also (AI) systems which improve an existing task or just enable one, can and are used for cost savings. For instance, the British Airline E a s y j e t   u s e s   (A I) systems to better predict the demand of food and beverage on its flights. It reduced the inventory costs for the airline and help it to sustain a cost advantage (Emarkerer , 2017).

Hence, future robotic may be applied to apartment service industry in hotels, instead of travel agents or airport services. For example, vending machines are found in public locations are doing the work of a hospitality workers and ATM machines have largely replaced the human labor of the bank teller. The design of robot-friendly hospitality facilities may bring cost benefit of adoption of robots for travel, tourism and hospitality companies. They are service robots.

In tourism service industry, customer attitudes can be influences in the mind of the tourist and is considered as an important element to influence the hotel, travel agent, airport services success. So service robotic participation will influence service robotic can bring positive attitude to their customers, such as providing excellent service for hotel book room service, air ticket check in /out service for airport travelers or apartment choice service for tourist journey arrangement choice services.

Thus, (AI)service will influence the country's overall hotel room booking, travel leisure and airport check in arrival service to let oversea tourists feel this country's tourism service can provide the most excellent service arrangement to compare other countries' travelling services. When, service robotic can be participated to the country's overall tourism related services, e.g. service robots will be faster than human employees, robots will deal with calculations better than human employees, robotic will provide more accurate information than human employees, robotic will be friendlier than human employees, robots will be more polite than human employees, robots will be able to understand guest's level of satisfaction, robot can understand more clear to any questions or orders to compare human employees.

Robotic can do special requests, they work not only in a programmed frame. Moreover, when any hotel livers can be influenced to have positive attitude towards the potential use of robotic in hotels, such as being served by robotic will be a memorable experience, being served by robots will be a pleasurable experience, being served by robots will be an existing experience, preference towards the appearance of the robots, preferences towards . To compare the human employees-robots performance ratio in a hotel, if they feel robotic performance can let them to feel better service to compare human employees, then the tourists will choose the hotel to live again, when they come back to the country to travel. So, it seems that future hotels ought may choose service robots to help them to serve their clients, if they can train robotics to let hotel guests to feel more satisfactory service feeling. Their hotel service tasks may include that the reception, multi-lingual robots is a talking dinosaur , responsible for greeting, checking in and assisting guests. At the cloakroom, a robotic aim stores luggage , and porter robots carry them to the rooms, replacing a friendly , human receptionist with a robotic dinosaur may appear questionable for hospitality aficionados, but the concept may appear to be successful.

In travel bots application aspect, it may include these service robots, customer-service bots is usually incorporated for example, in the provider's website and their functions are limited to answering basic questions and assisting the user with navigating through the home page. Facebook chatbots is more interactive than customer-service bots, allowing a possibility to enter search and booking –related data using another interface, e.g. Expedia's or skyscanner's facebook, messager bots as well as the travel AIbots is such applications still rely on instance messaging to interface with the customer , but also utilize algorithms and access to information to make recommendations, e.g. a virtual travel agent uses calendar and email information to produce personalized recommendations. In conclusion, all of the above service robots will be entertained for purposes in tourism mainly due to their efficiency and reliability asnd providing excellent service performance to compare human service employees in possible , when a number of the sbove mentional technologies are already a reality in tourism, they ought not appear counter-intuitive and unsuitable for service-encounters.

I believe automation in tourism service can bring new enjoyment exciting feeling to future dream-inspiring hospitality of the tourism -sector. We also need to believe tourists will be willing to adopt interact with service robots during their holidays and what is their perceived optimal trade off between efficiency and humanity.

(AI) raises driven automation industry development

1.1 (AI) - driven automation industry development how to influence work nature change

(AI) -driven automation industry will create wealth and expand economy growth to any countries, but it will be accompanied by changed in the skills that workers need to learn. One of main ways that technology increases productivity is by decreasing the number of labor hours needed to create a unit of output. It implies (AI) technology will influence low educated and low skillful labor number to be decreased (reduction employment number).

In contrast, technological change tended to work in a different direction throughout the nowadays. The advance of computer and the internet raised the relative productivity of higher skilled workers. So, routine-intensive occupations that focused on predictable tasks disappearance, such as switch board, operators, filming checkers, travel agents and assembling line workers etc. were particularly replaced by new technologies.

However, today, it may be challenging to predict exactly which jobs will be most immediately affected by (AI) driven-automation. The reason is because (AI) is not a single technology, but rather a collection of technologies that are felt unevenly through the economy to influence job changing both negatively and positively. In positively view point, (AI) driven-automation will make many workers more productive and increase demand for certain skills. Consequently, new jobs are likely to be directly create in areas , such as the development and supervision of (AI) as well as indirectly created in a range of areas throughout the economy as higher incomes lead to expanded demand. Otherwise, in negatively view point, many traditional human needed (demand) skillful jobs will be threatened by automation are highly concentrated among lower-paid, lower-skilled and less -educated workers. It means automation will cause pressure on demand for this group, pressure and employment, if (AI) can replace the low skilled and less educated workers' jobs. Thus, (AI) will have negative influence to impact on the labor market.

(AI) capabilities will enable automation of some tasks that have long required human labor. Why can (AI) replace some simple human jobs? For example, advances in robotics are expanding machines' abilities to interact with and sharp the physical world. Combined , (AI) and robotics will give rise to smarter machines that can perform more sophisticated functions than ever before and brings more advantages that humans have exercised. This will permit automation of many tasks now performed by human workers and could change the shape of the labor market and human activity.

Reference

Emarketer 2017, " How EasyJet uses artificial intelligence to improve operations-eMarketer" Emarketer. Accessed Dec. 10

http://www.emarketer, com/article/how-easyjet-uses.

Artificial-intelligence-improve-operations/1014558.

Entris, Laura: 2017 " Delta· Jetblue flights to test facial recognition scaual Fortune." Fortune.com

accessed Dec. 2019. http://fortune.com/2017/06/01/jetblue-delta-boarding-checkin/
Stark, Hareld. 2017 " Amazon go, A cashierless convenience store
Now available near you' Forbes.com accessed Dec. 9
http://www, forbes. Com/sites/haroldstark/2017/11/20
introducing-amazon-go-a-cashierless-convenience-
store-available-near you/20efofo952f9.

Bibliography

Adrian, P. (2012). Introduction to marketing theory & practice,
3 rd edition, London: Oxford press.

Ajzen, I (1991). The theory of planned behavior. Organizational behavior and human decision processes, 50(2), 179-211. doi: 10.1016/0749.5978 (91) 90020-7.
    Alba, Joseph W. and J. Wesley Hutchinson (1987). " Dimensions Of Consumer Expertise", Journal of consumer research, 13 March, 411-454.

Bailey, L., Mokhtarian, P.L. Little, A. (2008). The broader Connection Between Public Transportation, Energy Conservation And Greenhouse Gas Reduction, Report Prepared As Part Of TCRP Project J-11/Tasks Transit Cooperative Research Program, Transportation Research Board Submitted To American Public Transportation Association in
http://www.apta.com/research/into/online/land_use.cfmi, accessed 17 April 2008.
    Baucer, R,"Consumer Bhavior As Risk Taking , In Risk Taking And Information handling In Consumer Behavior", D. Coxceds Harvard University Press, Cambridge, Mass 1976.
    Biederman, P. (2008). Travel and tourism, Pearson Prentice Hall, New Jersey.
    Bogers, R. P., Brug, J. Van Assema, P., & Dagnetie, P.C.
(2004) , Explaining fruit and vegetable consumption: The theory of planned behavior and misconception of personal intake level. Appetite, 42,157-166.
    Bolton, Ruth N. (1998), " A Dynamic Model Of The Duration Of The Customer's Relationship With A Continuous Service Provider: The Role Of Satisfaction", Marketing Science, 17 (1), 45-65.

B.Shiv and A. Fedorikhin, " Heart And Min In Conflict: The Interplay Of affect And Cognition In Consumer Decision Making", J. Consumer Res., vol. 26, pp. 278-292, Dec. 1999.

Brown, K.W., Ryan, R.M. Reswell , J.D. (2007). Mindfulness: Theoretical Foundatins And Evidence For Its Salutary Effects. Psychological Inquiry, 18, 211-237.

Burke, R.R. : Behavioral effects of digital signage, J. Advertising Res. 49(2), 180-185 (2009).

Cant, M., Brink , A. & Brijall, S., Consumer behavior, Cape Town, South Africa: Juta, 2006.

Conner, M. & Abraham, C. (2001). Conscientiousness and the theory of planned behavior: Toward a more complete model of the antecedents of intention and behavior. Social psychology bulletin, 27, 1547-1561.

Cooper C. Mallon, K, Leadbetter S, Pollack L, Peipins (2005) , cancer internet search activity on a major search engine, United States 2001 to 2003, J Med Internet Res. 7(3): e36.

Cope, R. R. Cope and H. Davis (2008). Disney's virtual Queues: A strategic opportunity to co-brand services ? Journal of Business & economics research, vol. 6 no10, 13-20.

Cornelia, B.F. (1999) Rural development news, the North Central Regional Center For Rural Development vol. no 24 , IOWA.

Couper, M.P. J. Blair and T. Triplet (1999). A Comparison Of Mail And E-mail For a Survey Of Employees In USA Statistical Agencies. Journal Of Official Statistics, 15, 39-56.

David J. Nowak & Gordon M. Melsler (2016) " Air quality effects of urban trees and parks." National recreation and park association, USA.

Data monitor (2008). The proctor and gamble company. Retrieved Nov. 15 2009 from http://www.datamonitor.com/

De Hollander, A. E. M., J.M. Melse, Elebret & P. G.N. Kramers (1999), " An Aggregate public health indicator to represent the impact of multiple environmental exposures" Epidemiology: 606-617.

De Visser, R.O., & McDonnell, E.J. (2013). " Man points": Masculine capital and young men's health. Health psychology, 32(1), 5-14. doi:10. 1037/a0029045.

Dunn, J & A Neumsister (2002). Knowledge management in the Information age. E. business review, Fall , 37-45. Jounral of service, spring 2011, vol. 4, no1, De Grovte (2009).

Dyer, D., F. Dalzell & R. Olegario (2004). Rising tide. Lessons learned from 165 years of brand building at Procter and Gamble. Boston, MA: Havard Business School Press.

Eysenbach G (2006) Infodemiology: Tracking flu- related searches on the web for syndromic surveillance. American Medical Informatics Associaion Annual Symposium Proceedings , Curran Associates, Red Hook, NY, pp. 244-248.

Ettredge M, Gerdes, J. Karuga , G (2005) Using web- based search data to predict macro-economic statistics. Commun ACM 48: 87-92.

Felce, D. and Perry, J. (1995). Quality of life: A contribution to its definition and measurement, vol. 16, no.1 pp: 51-74.

Feldman, Jack M. And John G. Lynch Jr. (1988), "Self-
Generated Validity And Other Effects Of Measurement On Belife, Attitude, Intention And Behavior", Journal of applied psychology, 73(3),421-35.

Fiese, M, Hofmann, W., & Wanke, M (2009). The impulsive consumer. Predicting consumer behavior with implicit reaction time measurement. In M. Wanke (ed.) Social psychology of consumer behavior (pp.335-364). New York, NY: Psychology press.

Fitzsimons, Gavan, J. And Vicki G. Morwitz (1996), " The Effect Of Measuring Intent On Brand-Level
Purchase Behavior", Journal of consumer research, 23 (1), 1-11.

Hallerman , D. (2008) video Advertising Online: Spending And Pricing , New York. E-Marketer.

Harriet Griffey. (2010) The art of concentration, enhance focus, Reduce, stress and achieve move. Macmillan publishers ltd,Basinastoke and Oxford, London UK.

Helleman, D. (2008) Video Advertising Online: Spending And Pricing , New York, E-Marketer.

Hensen, C. (2003). Kreuzfahrtourismus.www.christoph- hensen.de/ Facharbeit.pdf.

Huang, H.I. (2012). An empirical analysis of the strategic Management of competitive advantage: a case study of higher technical and vocational education in Taiwan (Doctoral dissertation,

Victoria University).

Jamieson, Linda F. And Frank M. Bass (1989), " Adjusting Stated Intention Measures To Predict Trial Purchase Of New Products: A Comparison Of Models And Methods," Journal of marketing research, 26 (August), 336-45.

Korea Ministry Of Environment. Public Organizations spend 2.2 Trillon Korean Won To Purchase green Products in 2014; Ministry Of Environment: Sejoung, Korea, 2015.

Kremers, S.P. J., De Bruijn, G.J., droomers, M., Van Lenthe, F. J., & Brug, J. (2005). Environmental interventions for selected dietary behaviors in adults. In J. Brug & F. J. Van Lenthe (eds.) , Environmental determinants and interventions for physical activity, nutrition and smoking: A review pp. 282-315. Rotterdam: Erasmus Medical Center.

Lee, D.; Kim, M. ; Lee, J. adoption of green electricity policies: Investigating the role of environmental attitudes via big data-driven search-queries. Energy policy 2016. 90, 187-201.

Lee, Terrence, " Tech in Asia-connecting Asia's startup system " Tech. in Asia- connecting Asia's startup ecosystem, N.p.,4 July 2016.

Los Angeles Country Department Of public Health (2016), Country Health Ranking Model, Retrieved From www.countryhealthrankgings.org/our-approach. USA.

Mayne, Lonnie. " Evolve of die in the age of the consumer". Entrepreneur, N.P. , 16 Apr. 2014. web of Oct. 2016.

McGregor, S.L. T., & Goldsmith, E.B. (1998). Expanding our understanding of quality of life, standard of living and well-being. Journal of family and consumer science, 90(2), 2-6, 22.

McMichael, A.J. M. Mckee, J. Shkolnikov and T. Valkanen (2004), " Morality trends and setbacks, global convergence or divergence?", Lancet 363, 1155-1159.

Melse, J.M. & A.E. M. De Hollander (2001). " Human Health And The Environment", background document for the OECD Environmental Outlook, OECD, Paris.

Moschis, George p. & Roy, L. Moore (1979), " Decision making among the young. A socialization perspective " Journal of consumer research , 6 (September).

Mulligan, M. Banerjee, T & Thomas, N. (2008) ,European Paid Content And Activity Forecast, (2008 to 2013), Jupiter Research.

Peter, J., Ryan, M, M, " An Investigation Of Perceived Risk At The Brand Level, " Journal of marketing research, 13 May 1976, pp. 184-188.

Pieters, R., & Wedel, M. (2007). Goal Control Of Visual Attention To Advertising: The Yarbus Implication. Journal Of Consumer Research, 34, 224-233 (August).

Parasuaman, and Leonard L. Berry (1985), " Problems And Strategies In Sevices Marketing", Journal of marketing, 49 (Spring), 33-46.

Priesnitz, W. (2007) Counting Our Food Miles. Natural Life, 1 July.

R.C. Oliver, " When is consumer loyalty?" J.Marketing vol. 63, pp.33-44.1999.

Reggiani, A . (ed). 1998, accessibility, trade and locational behavior, Ashgate publishing ltd, England.

Rushe, D. (2013) " The 10 best paid CEO in America". The Guardian , 22 Oct, (online). Available at:
http://www.theguardian.com/business/2013/Oct22/best-paid-chief-executives-america (Accessed: 3 May 2014).

Spiekermann and Wegener (2007), update of selected potential accessibility indicators. Final report, urban and regional research (S&W), RRG spatial planning and geoinformation. ESPON. Available online
at http:// <www.espon.eu/mmp/online/website/ contentprojects/947/ 1297/file_2724/espon_accessibility_update-2006-fr_070207.pdf>, accessed on 1 July 2009.

Starbucks (2014) Our company available at http:// www. starbucks.com/about- us/company-information (accessed: 3 May 2014).

Shostack, G. Lynn (1984), " Designing Services That Deliver", Harvard Business Review, 62 (January-February), 133-9.

Shostack, G. Lynn (1985), " Planning The Service Encounter ,in the service encounter" , John A. Czepiel, Michael R. Solomon, and Carol F. Suprenant, eds. New York: Lexington Books, 243-54.

Shostack, G. Lynn (1987), " Service Positioning Through, Structural Change", Journal of marketing, 51 (Janurary), 34-43.

Soloman, Michael R. (1985), "Packaging The Service Provider", Service Industries Journal , 5(1), 64-71.

Stevens, C.W. (1980), "K-MartStores Try New Look To Invite More Spending" The Wall Street Journal, Nov. 26, 29-35.

Sullivan, Nicholas P(2007). You can hear me now: How Micro loans and cell phones are connecting the world, San Francisco, CA: John Wilsey & Sans, 2007.

T. Ambler, A. Ioannides, And S. Rose, " Brand s On The Brain : Neuroimages Of Advertising ", Business Strategy rev., vol. 11, 3. pp. 17-30. 2000.

Westbrook, Robert A. (1980), " Intrapersonal affective influences on consumer satisfaction with products, " Journal of consumer research , 7 (June) 49-54.

Wiig, k.(1993). Knowledge management foundations: Thinking About thinking. How people and organizations create, represent and use knowledge vol.1 , of knowledge management series schema press: Arlington, TX.

World Health Organization (2003). Diet, nutrition and the prevention of Chronic diseases report of a joint WHO/FAO. expert consultation. Geneva: World Health Organization.

Wysocki, B. (1979), " Sight, Smell, Sound: They're all arms in retailer's arsenal" The Wall Street Journal, Nov. 17, 1979. 1-35.

Yale Center For Environmental Law And Policy (2006). Environmental Performance Index. Data available on-line at http://epi.yale.edu